the Friend *of the* Bridegroom

Spiritual
Direction
and the
Encounter
With Christ

the Friend *of the* Bridegroom

Thomas H. Green, S.J.

ave maria press   Notre Dame, IN

Imprimi Potest: The Reverend Romeo J. Intengan, S.J.
    Provincial Superior, Philippine Province
    October 18, 1999
Nihil Obstat: The Reverend Monsignor Socrates B. Villegas
Imprimatur: Jaime Cardinal Sin, DD
    Archbishop of Manila
    Given at Manila on 18 September, 1999
The *Nihil Obstat* and *Imprimatur* are official declarations that a book or pamphlet is free of doctrinal or moral error. No implication is contained therein that those who have granted the *Nihil Obstat* and *Imprimatur* agree with its contents, opinions, or statements expressed.
Scripture quotations are from the *Today's English Version Bible*, copyright © American Bible Society, 1966, 1971, 1976, 1992.

International Standard Book Number: 0-87793-938-1
Cover and text design by Brian C. Conley
Printed and bound in the United States of America.
Library of Congress Cataloging-in-Publication Data

Green, Thomas H. (Thomas Henry), 1932-
    The friend of the bridegroom : spiritual direction and the encounter with Christ / Thomas H. Green.
        p. cm.
    Includes bibliographical references.
    ISBN 0-87793-938-1 (pbk.)
    1. Spiritual direction. I. Title.
BX2350.7 .G74   2000
253.5'3--dc21

                                    00-008685
                                        CIP

Contents

Introduction

Spiritual direction has been of central importance in my busy pastoral life. As I look back on the years of my Jesuit formation and my priestly ministry, I realize how important the surprising movements of God have been in my life. One of the divine surprises that was most significant was my 1970 appointment to San Jose Seminary in Manila to assist in the work of spiritual direction. Now, on the occasion of my golden jubilee as a Jesuit and as I complete thirty years at San Jose, that work continues. Woven through the work of spiritual direction were courses in pastoral theology that I taught at the Loyola School of Theology, which led in turn to my eight books in the area of spirituality. I wrote on topics such as prayer, discernment, and lay spirituality, but the one area that was always on the horizon, which I am now addressing, is spiritual direction.

Spiritual direction is an important element of the Christian life. The mature Christianity to which the Second Vatican Council called us, laity and clergy alike, requires solid formation and an inner-directed spirituality. This inner-directed spirituality is not an effort to escape from the world, but to find God in this very place and time where we are called to love and serve him.

I am often asked if the book is for directees or for directors. I try, actually, to focus on the relationship between director and directee, with the Holy Spirit as the essential third party. It could be said that Chapters One to Three are more directee-centered, while Four, Five, and the Epilogue focus on the director. In every case, however, I envision three parties: director, directee, and the Holy Spirit, each one listening and learning from the conversation between the other two.

The title *The Friend of the Bridegroom* came from the central insight that St. John the Baptist, who described himself thus (Jn 3: 29), is the ideal model for a good spiritual director. His joyful acceptance of the subordinate role he played in the drama of the messiah's coming should guide the director in his or her joyful acceptance of a similar role today.

I dedicate this work to all those who have trusted me, whether as director or directee. Later we will hear one of my directors saying that this is the greatest compliment one person can pay another. I feel it is so, and I am greatly honored.

The Contemporary Context of Spiritual Direction

Father Baltazar Alvarez became St. Teresa of Avila's spiritual director in 1559. She was then about forty-five years old, and he, a Jesuit recently ordained, was some twenty years her junior. Between then and the foundation of the first convent of the Carmelite reform in August, 1562, Alvarez was a great support to her in the face of much opposition from the religious and secular powers.

Sometime in 1561, however, when Teresa was censured and told to abandon the reform, Alvarez must have lost his nerve. Teresa tells us in her autobiography (Chapter 33) that she found peace despite all the opposition she was facing. The Lord assured her that it was his project and he would see to its realization. And yet:

> What troubled me a great deal was that on one occasion my confessor (Alvarez) wrote me a letter . . . which suggested that in some way I had been acting against his wishes. . . . [This came] from the source which would cause me the greatest pain. For, amid this multitude of persecutions, my confessor, whom I had

expected to console me, wrote that . . . all that had happened was just a dream and that henceforth . . . I must
not try to do anything more of the kind or talk about it
any more. . . .[1]

I mention this famous incident here because I believe
it reveals the sea change of perspective from the
medieval idea of spiritual direction to that of our day.
Teresa obeyed Alvarez, as the Lord commanded, and the
incident made clear to one of the strongest women in the
history of the Church that the project of reforming
Carmel must be the Lord's work and not hers. It was up
to him to convince the powers-that-be. And she says later
that Alvarez and St. John of the Cross were the best of the
many spiritual directors she had in her lifetime.

My point is that, in her day, spiritual direction was
obediential. The director, as had been true for centuries,
was an authority figure to be obeyed. Alvarez and John
served Teresa well. And yet, if a woman of her quality
came to me for spiritual direction today, I would not be
disposed—not even able, in fact!—to *command* her to
abandon (or continue) the reform. The ideal of direction,
and the perception of the role of the spiritual director, has
changed significantly, especially since Vatican II.

What is this new perception? We still recognize the
value of authority and obedience in the Christian life.
But the director is not a superior. He or she is, we might
say, a facilitator, a co-discerner, an interpreter, somewhat
like a medical diagnostician. It is the purpose of this
book to clarify what this means. In so doing, I would like
to reflect on my experience of spiritual direction—both
as a directee, for some fifty years, and as director for the
past thirty-five years. The book is intended to be experi-
ential rather than theoretical. That is, while I will refer to

some of the good and growing collection of works on the theory, my personal concern is with the practice as I have experienced it.

For almost twenty-five years, I have been offering a course on discernment at the Loyola School of Theology in Manila.[2] In more recent years, I have titled the course "Discernment and Spiritual Direction"—expressing my conviction that the work of discernment is at the heart of the task of the spiritual director. Moreover, since I see the director's role as facilitative rather than directive, I begin the course with a short essay by George Aschenbrenner, S.J., (the author of the landmark article, "Consciousness Examen") entitled "A Contemporary Approach to Spiritual Formation in Religious Life."[3] It helps my students to situate spiritual direction and discernment within the contemporary perspective of which I spoke above. Although Fr. Aschenbrenner's specific concern is with initial formation in a religious community—reflecting the fact that he was a Jesuit novice-master for many years—I believe his essential vision is equally valid for any committed Christian today. For this reason, I would like to share with you, as we begin our discussion of spiritual direction, the main ideas he proposes.

"Novitiate" vs. "Noviceship"

Aschenbrenner begins his article by contrasting two approaches to formation, which he calls "novitiate" and "noviceship." "Novitiate usually means a building where men and women in training stay for a year or two, but noviceship means a process and not a building." Novitiate, the building, symbolizes the "external structures which before gave direction, order and unity to the formation program." In a novitiate the emphasis is on conformity to external structures. The good novice is the one who follows all the rules: who is always on time for prayer, liturgy, and meals; who does her work faithfully and well; who obeys and does not challenge authority.

As Aschenbrenner says, he (and I and all our generation) experienced a novitiate formation. Given the huge number of vocations fifty years ago, that was perhaps inevitable. In my novitiate, there were 130 novices in two years. Personal, one-to-one contact with the novice-master would have been virtually impossible. So the authenticity of our vocation was judged mainly by how well we fit in to the structures of Jesuit life. We young Jesuits spoke of "the long black line" as symbolic of our Jesuit identity.[4] And even fourteen years later, when I was preparing for ordination, the professor gave us this criterion for a worthy celebration of the eucharist: when we left the altar, the congregation should not have noticed which priest celebrated the Mass. That sounds incredible in the light of our renewed liturgy today, but in 1963 it was accepted as the norm (though not always without question, since Vatican II was in progress).

As Aschenbrenner notes, "when I passed through it [the novitiate process] . . . I did not find much difficulty with it." He is still a friend of mine, and I can attest that he is a happy, well-adjusted person who has a very positive effect on the men and women whose lives he touches. But his point in the article—especially in the light of his many years as novice-master—is that "in view of what is happening in today's world . . . we cannot continue to follow past methods." Most of the externally imposed structures (and I believe the same would be true to a large extent in raising a family today—at least when the children reach adolescence) have disappeared.

What, then, can replace novitiate structures? This is where Aschenbrenner proposes the noviceship model as an alternative. What is it? "Noviceship is basically a matter of spiritual formation, and involves the radical reorientation of the whole person, down to the roots of one's being and the effective center of one's consciousness." Thus noviceship, by contrast with novitiate, focuses not on external structures but on the inner dynamics of the person's identity and growth. In noviceship, the person is asked to look within—to question not only external performance but inner motives. Why do I do what I do? Why do I react to others in the way that I do? What do I really think of myself and of God?

Noviceship as Challenging, Even Threatening

The struggle to conform to external structures is difficult enough. My first months as a Jesuit novice were a painful adjustment to a new set of structures quite alien to my life at home. But much more difficult is the challenge to honestly confront myself. As Aschenbrenner says: "This radical reorientation is not easy for anyone. In practice, a man or woman is asked to be in a very healthy way suspicious and distrustful of every aspect of the motivation behind their actions, to be willing to explore and reorient this motivation."

Although I did not realize it at the time, this challenge was at the heart of my struggles in those early months as a Jesuit novice in 1949. I thought my problem was caused by my being a Rochesterian from upstate New York who had not known any Jesuits before entering, thrust into a world of sophisticated New York City men, almost all from Jesuit schools. But hindsight has taught me that something much deeper was involved. I was a reluctant candidate for the Jesuits. That is, I applied for admission because I could not get the Lord "off my back." I had a girlfriend and a scholarship to college and medical school—and these were much more attractive to me. But there was an inner unease, which I hoped would be cured by applying for the seminary—and being rejected! You can imagine my disappointment when I was accepted. It was a compliment, of course, but the cost was too high.

I spent the first four months of the novitiate trying to persuade the novice-master to send me home. I wanted to leave, but I wanted the decision to come from the Lord. Fortunately, the novice-master refused to play my game. He told me I was free to leave at any time, but that I should be honest enough to admit why I was leaving: not because I did not have a vocation, but because I did not want to accept it. As I have told countless participants in vocation seminars in the Philippines, a religious vocation (like marriage) is an invitation, not a command. We are free to accept or decline it, and the Lord will still love us. But we have to have the courage, and the maturity, to make the decision for ourselves.

The Kind of Person Required for Noviceship

As I reflect on my experience now, I can see how difficult Aschenbrenner's "radical reorientation" was for me at seventeen. Without my realizing it, the novice-master was asking me "to be in a very healthy way suspicious and distrustful of every aspect" of my motivation, and "to explore and reorient this motivation."

The struggle was painful, and I was not very graceful about it, but it seems—judging from the fact I am happy and still a Jesuit fifty years later—that there were within me the resources to confront my own real motivation.

What resources were needed? I had to get free of my own attachments, to open myself to a new world of experience and growth. That did not happen overnight, of course, but after about four months I realized that I really did want to stay in the novitiate. There would be many struggles in the years to follow, but now they were the fruit of my own choosing. I was not "seduced" by God after all.

When discussing the qualities needed to undergo the noviceship formation, Aschenbrenner mentions first "a profound self-acceptance and self-confidence." That is a tall order at the age of seventeen. But I had come from a loving family, and had been affirmed by them and by my friends along the way. Good vocations, I have often said, normally come from happy homes.[5] Grace can work in the most unpromising of human situations; but how much easier it is "to suspect and to distrust in a healthy way one's motivation, so that the desired reorientation can take place," if we are secure in our identity and in the fact that we are loved.

If the person is not ready for this challenge of self-confrontation, "a process that is calculated to be formative becomes destructive." I think this is why the church does not favor hasty (especially teenage) marriages, and why most religious communities would rarely accept a candidate at seventeen today. In the novitiate model of the past, it was easier to shape the tree (to external patterns of behavior) if you started early. But for noviceship and the self-questioning it entails—which is painful at its best—much greater maturity is needed.

Maturity, self-acceptance, the willingness to confront one's inner contradictions and ambiguities, and a sincere desire to find God's will for one's life are the characteristics required for undergoing the noviceship process. This is not limited to religious life, but is crucial to any genuine experience of spiritual direction.

The Kind of Person Produced by Noviceship

Given the challenge and the cost, why would the noviceship process be much more acceptable today? We are in a time of transition in the Philippines: not every religious community, even now, accepts (or even understands) the "noviceship" ideal. But it is becoming more and more the norm. The Philippine bishops, for example, are realizing the importance of producing priests who are mature, stable, and solid in their commitment to the celibate life of service. Ordination normally comes at a later age today, and various means (some of which we will discuss in the following sections) are employed to foster maturity and responsible love and service.

We in the Philippines are realizing by experience the truth of what Aschenbrenner wrote some twenty-five years ago:

> This approach will produce men and women who are inner-directed, interiorly reliable and dependable. When such persons want to know what they should do now, and which course of action to follow, they do not look around to see what others are doing, but they look inside themselves for answers.

Could one be such a person at the age of seventeen? Probably not. I realize now that I judged as good and "holy" those novices who in my eyes appeared to be such. As time passed and a number of the "holy" ones left the novitiate, I was forced to look deeper into my own motivation and to realize that my vocation was a very personal call and challenge.

Even pleasing the novice-master could not be my goal. I remember one occasion when he told us in a conference that we should be completely open to him. Since he was a challenging, even threatening figure for me, I found the prospect very intimidating. But I wanted to be a good novice, so I screwed my courage to the sticking point and went in to tell him my inner struggles. I cannot recall today what I told him; his reaction, however, is etched on my mind forever. As I told my tale of woe, he sat back in his chair and made a gesture I had never seen before, but whose meaning I immediately recognized. He started bowing an imaginary violin—and I knew what he meant: "Sad, sad story!" That is, "Be a man and not a baby. Don't feel so sorry for yourself." There was wisdom in his admonition, but the immediate effect on me was traumatic. Despite my desire to be a good novice, I resolved that I would never open up to him again—even if my eternal salvation depended on it!

As I look back now, that was a graced moment of maturing for me—although perhaps not in the way the novice-master intended it. I gradually realized, as my hurt feelings subsided, that I could not find my self-worth in the approval of any human being. And the lesson was reinforced by an experience during my first years as a young seminarian in the Philippines. I had difficulty with my rector in the school where I was teaching and prefecting boarding students. The worst part was that I could not figure out what the problem was. Much as I wanted to please him, things went from bad to worse. The climax came when he told me one day: "Maybe you think I don't like you. But don't worry. When I myself was a young scholastic, my rector said to me: 'If I have my way, you will never be ordained.' And look at me now: not only was I ordained, but I am now the rector. So someday you can be rector too!"

I had grown a bit since my novitiate days, and so I replied: "Father, I don't want to be rector. I just want to know what displeases you." I never really got the answer to that question. But I saw even more clearly that I needed to be true to myself, and that the Lord's opinion of me had to be the one that mattered. He can—and often does—speak to me through others. But I cannot accept their opinions blindly. I have to bring them back to the Lord, and discover in discerning prayer what *he* is saying to me through others.[6]

I share these personal experiences only in order to enflesh what Aschenbrenner has said: "When such persons want to know what they should do now, . . . they do not look around to see what others are doing, but they look inside themselves for answers." That is what the Lord was teaching me in these painful experiences. Fortunately, however, not all the means he uses are painful. In that first assignment in the Philippines, there were other priests who affirmed me, and helped me to realize that perhaps the rector had problems of his own; perhaps the difficulty was not wholly with me but largely with him. And over the years of formation I was blessed with good spiritual directors, who encouraged me to be true to myself. Several years later, one man, to whom I am eternally grateful, listened to my story of my inner darkness at prayer, then said: "I must admit that I do not understand what is happening to you. But I feel sure it is the Lord working." That was all I needed. If he, a man of God, felt I was on the right track, then I could journey on in peace, even though I (and he) did not understand what was happening.

Inner-directed and God-directed: this is what the Lord seeks to make us through the experiences, painful and joyful, of our religious formation. As Aschenbrenner says about the person produced by a noviceship formation: "They have learned through experience and conversion of heart to recognize selfishness, and to distinguish self-centeredness from a God-centered way of life. This is the characteristic of an inner-directed, interiorly reliable person, who is flexible, adaptable, and ready to do almost anything."

The Means to Achieve a Noviceship Formation

We realize today that formation in Christ is a lifelong process. From the noviceship perspective, it is clear why this is so. We are always on the way to becoming inner-directed, God-centered persons. As I explained in *When the Well Runs Dry*, there are essentially three stages of human love and interior growth: getting to know (courtship), loving (honeymoon), and truly loving (midlife). John of the Cross calls the last stage the "dark night." Using a term suggested by Teresa of Avila, I called it the "dry well." This dark night or dry well is the ultimate stage in the ongoing transformation of which St. Paul speaks so beautifully (Phil 3:12-14): "I do not claim that I have already succeeded or have already become perfect. I keep striving to win the prize for which Christ Jesus has already won me to himself. . . . So I run straight toward the goal in order to win the prize, which is God's call through Christ Jesus to the life above."

Given the basic attitudes of openness, self-acceptance, interiority, and God-centeredness, what means can assist in the noviceship process of formation? Aschenbrenner cites three: life in a community of faith and prayer, realistic apostolic exposure, and regular spiritual direction "with openness and trust." Let us say a word about each of the three:

1. Life in a community of faith and prayer. Aschenbrenner speaks of the community dimension of our formation as "education by osmosis." We are, by nature and by grace, persons in community. By nature we learn our values, our ways of loving and acting, from the communities in which we are formed; but also, and especially, by grace. As I have reflected on the central mystery of our faith, the Holy Trinity, this is what it has come to mean to me. From all eternity our God is community: three Persons in one God. God has never been able to say "I"—it has always been "We." And our vocation is to enter into the community, the family of God. Concretely, this means that community life is an essential element in Christian formation. This is why the family is the "nuclear church"—and why, as we said earlier, good religious (and marital) vocations normally come from good families.

But children are given to their parents on loan for twenty years. Then they move on and form their own communities. And yet grandparents, and adults in general, still have a need for community, if they are to continue to mature in their faith. The worshipping community gathered at the eucharist should play a crucial formative role. Also, for many today, lay prayer communities are a significant factor in the process of maturing in faith and love. While the charismatic movement has been of great value here, not all prayer communities are (or should be) charismatic. In the Philippines I know of Christian Life Community groups, faith sharing groups, parish Bible study groups. And the movement known as Basic Ecclesial Communities (BECs) or Basic Christian Communities has been a significant tool in deepening faith and social concern ("a faith which does justice"), especially in areas where the people/priest ratio is very high.

Seminary formation reflects the same growing realization of the importance of the community dimension. San Jose Seminary is now divided into BECs, smaller groupings of eight to ten seminarians living together on the same floor, praying together, sharing apostolate, and generally forming bonds that last long after they leave the seminary.[7]

But whether in the lay life or in the seminary or convent, what is crucial is the formative value of community. Aschenbrenner says: "As they deal with one another, they educate and form one another in a way a director is not able to. Faced with such circumstances, it is very important that every effort be made to provide a community of faith and prayer, within which those persons may live and grow." In the rest of the book we will stress the central role of the spiritual director, but still I would agree with Aschenbrenner that community is an essential complement to the work of spiritual direction.

2. Realistic apostolic exposure. The second element Aschenbrenner sees as important is experience "in realistic apostolic situations, where the novices are much more on their own, away from the novitiate building and away from the spiritual director." This on-the-job training gives them an opportunity "to see whether . . . they are able to carry out what they have been talking, praying and reflecting about." Specifically, it helps them to test the realism and the depth of their paschal faith. Such exposure is clearly present in the lay life, or at least the opportunities for it are all around us. Parents could be too protective of their children, just as they could be too lenient too early. The challenge is to find the proper balance and to sense the appropriate time to allow the young person to try her wings and test her own resources.

I recall my mother saying more than once when I was visiting her in Rochester: "I don't understand why you, the sentimental one in the family, have to live so far away. If you care so much about what is happening to everyone, why don't you stay home?" She had read me well; family ties are very important to me. I had not volunteered for the missions because I was unhappy in my own country, but because I sensed the Lord calling me to "a strange land." I did not, however, have the opportunity to explain this to her. After a short pause, she answered her own question: "However, your father and I raised you to be independent, and I suppose I should be happy that we succeeded!" As I reflected on this in the years that followed, I realized how true it was. We were encouraged to express our opinions at the dinner table, to involve ourselves in school and parish activities, and to do useful work. I delivered 100 newspapers daily at 6 a.m. for four years, and then, in my senior year in high school, worked as a delivery boy in the men's clothing section of a local department store.

Aschenbrenner's specific concern is with formation for religious life. Our formation was quite cloistered during the first seven years of Jesuit life. We did have apostolic exposure at that time; but it was very limited. I have said in later years that when I finished philosophical (college) studies and went to Cagayan de Oro for my teaching regency, I had to discover all over again what girls looked like. It is against that background that he stresses "experiences in realistic apostolic situations." The danger was that, even with a healthy home environment, seminarians could regress, personally and in a realistic faith, if their formation was in a hermetically sealed environment.

Like most seminaries and convent formation houses, we at San Jose Seminary have come to realize that today. Our seminarians are much more on their own (in BEC groups) for their overnight weekend apostolate in the squatter areas. They study their theology not at San Jose but in the Loyola School of Theology, along with young men from several religious congregations—and a student body that is about fifty percent women, both sisters and laity, married and single. Whatever problems they may have, they will not have to discover all over again what girls look like!

Also, for about twenty-five years now we have had an extra year of formation, called the Spiritual Pastoral Formation Year (SPFY). Placed between the second and third years of theology, it is, in effect, a novitiate year for diocesan seminarians. The high point for the men is the thirty-day Ignatian retreat. But they also have numerous workshops on psycho-spiritual integration (including modules on sexuality and celibacy), and they have two four to six week exposure programs. In the first, they live with a family in a remote rural area, sharing (often in a crowded one-room hut) their food, their farm work, and their social life. The second is an urban exposure: they work at menial jobs, sharing the life of the urban poor, known as seminarians only to the one who employed them.

What precisely is the value of such experiences? As Aschenbrenner says well, "to be outside the novitiate building and set in the middle of life's trying situations, to feel the eyes of the world on you, to have people poke fun at you, to be judged as strange and odd, that is a great challenge." Can I still be a person of faith, even in a skeptical environment? Can I serve in a spirit of faith those who do not understand my calling or the reason for my service? To recall my own youth, I could never have learned at home the lessons of my newspaper route (the customers who tried to avoid paying me, or the single man who, when I went for my weekly collections, asked me questions about my sexuality which I did not understand) or my work in a department store (where the salesmen, nice men generally, enjoyed shocking me and my teenage co-worker with their stories of sexual conquest). Those things never happened—nor were they talked about—at home!

3. *Regular spiritual direction with openness and trust.* How did the questions of the lonely bachelor and the sly talk of the clothing salesmen affect me? I was puzzled, troubled. Exposure to the world and life in community are not an unmixed good. We live in a world of darkness and light. The challenge is to sort the darkness from the light. And this is why the spiritual director is the crucial person in an open noviceship formation. As Aschenbrenner asks earlier in his article, "what will prevent the series of experiences and atmospheres

connected with this process from becoming chaotic, and therefore not formative but destructive?"

If we grant that exposure to the real world is essential for maturing, then equally important is the help of a good guide, an interpreter, a spiritual director. I did not have a formal spiritual director as a youth. Fortunately, though, I did have a father and a mother with whom I could share my doubts and confusion. It was my father to whom I brought my puzzlement about the questions of the bachelor on my paper route. He told me, very simply, to keep my distance from the man and not to entertain his questions. He did not go into detail (that was not his style), but I realized clearly that I was on dangerous ground. At the same time, my father never suggested that I give up my paper route. Perhaps he trusted me to use good judgment and follow good advice. If so, it was an excellent preparation for my life-work as a spiritual director.

Conclusion

In discussing the role of the director in formation, Aschenbrenner says: "Humanly and patiently, the director invites the one he is directing to pursue the openness which this process requires." I take this to mean openness to the director—but also to experience, to what is happening within myself, and ultimately to the Lord. Thus the director is a wise companion on the journey of life. She or he helps me to interpret my own experience.

For this reason, the spiritual director is the crucial person in the noviceship model of formation. In the old novitiate pattern it was the superior or the parent as authority figure. If generous conformity is the ideal, then the most important formator is the one who gives me the pattern to conform to and enforces my adherence to it. But if honest confrontation with the inner truth of myself and of God speaking within me is the goal, then the role of the spiritual director is central and essential. Authority and external observance are still important. But, as my current rector at San Jose often points out to us on the faculty, he can only deal with the external observance. The more critical part of the process takes place in the one-to-one encounter of each man with his spiritual director. Only there can the crucial questions of motivation, sincerity, and an honest listening to the call of God to this person be addressed.

In the next chapter, I hope to explore in greater depth this crucial task of the spiritual director.

Question for Reflection and Sharing

Note: In the previous pages I have cited numerous examples from my own experience to clarify the points George Aschenbrenner makes in his important article. I would suggest the following for reflection and perhaps, as I do in my course on discernment and spiritual direction, for small-group sharing:

Was my own early formation—at home, in school, or in a religious community—more a novitiate or a noviceship? What kind of guidance do I look for in my life now as an adult?

The Role of the Spiritual Director

San Jose Seminary is on the campus of the Ateneo de Manila University. Our college seminarians study at the Ateneo before proceeding to the Loyola School of Theology. Thus they, along with the lay students, take basic theology courses as part of their college curriculum. One striking addition to the old lecture approach to theology is the requirement that they undergo, often on weekends, certain short-term exposures to the real life of the ordinary people of Manila and the rural areas. These are similar to, but shorter than, the Spiritual Pastoral Formation Year (SPFY) exposures that we mentioned in the previous chapter. While about twenty percent of our students (including the seminarians) are receiving financial aid, most come from the more affluent strata of Philippine society. Thus the exposure to life in squatter areas can be quite a shock. It brings them face to face with a style of life very different from what they knew at home.

What is the value of such immersion or exposure experiences? The hope is that their faith will be challenged, "conscientized." That is, that they will become aware of the needs of their fellow Filipinos, and will see their education not only as a privilege but as a responsibility. We hope they will become, in Fr. Pedro Arrupe's classic expression of the Jesuit ideal, "men and women for others." That is our hope; and often it is beautifully realized in their later lives of service to the country.

There is, however, a danger. As we have seen, Aschenbrenner expressed it as follows: "what will prevent the series of experiences . . . connected with this process from becoming chaotic, and therefore not formative but destructive?" The purpose of the exposure is not to challenge the students to change society *today*. If they so understood it, they could be moved to abandon, or to neglect, their studies. And then they would not have the skills needed to make a difference in the marketplace after they finish their education. Pursuing a short-term good could jeopardize their long-range contribution to the building of a just society.

What then is needed? The exposure is indeed valuable, *provided* they process their experience when they return to class. Their teachers have to help them to reflect on their experience, and to see what it really means to them and what their response should be. If this is done well, their initially chaotic experiences will be formative and not destructive.

In Chapter One we saw that this is a good analogy for the work of a spiritual director. Her or his role is to help the pray-er interpret her experiences—not just on a weekend exposure, but in the whole of her life—of God, and of his call to her in the real world in which she lives. In the present chapter, we wish to explore in more detail this description of the director's role.

Defining Spiritual Direction

Recent literature about spiritual direction reflects a fair consensus on its meaning. Let me cite just two definitions that I have found helpful. The first is given by William A. Barry, S.J., and William J. Connolly, S.J., in their influential book, *The Practice of Spiritual Direction.* Spiritual direction is "help given by one Christian to another, which enables that person to pay attention to God's personal communication to him or her, to respond to this personally communicating God, to grow in intimacy with this God, and to live out the consequences of the relationship."[1] Thus the focus of spiritual direction is on experience, specifically on religious experience, and not on ideas or speculative theology. The experience in question here is that of the *directee*, not of the director. The director's experience, as we shall see in Chapter Three, is very helpful in interpreting the directee's experience, but it is the latter that is to be interpreted. This will involve (to varying degrees, depending on the need of the directee) helping her to "pay attention," to hear God's word to her; to recognize, to understand the response the Lord is calling for; to be empowered to respond generously because of her growing "intimacy with this Lord," and thus "to live out the consequences of this relationship." To hear, to understand, to respond in love: these are the three moments of the directee's experience with which the director can help her.

Similarly, John Wright, S.J., in a monograph entitled "A Discussion on Spiritual Direction," describes spiritual direction as "an inter-personal situation, in which one person assists another to develop and come to maturity in the life of the spirit: that is, the life of faith, hope and love."[2] Wright ("to oversimplify very much") identifies faith with the directee's prayer life, hope with "his difficulties, sufferings, disappointments and problems," and love with "his life in the Christian community." The parallel with faith, hope, and love may be too simplistic and artificial, but Wright's description clearly shows that the subject matter of spiritual direction is the *whole* of the directee's life—not just her prayer life in a narrow sense.

Prayer is indeed the heart of the matter, just as the love-relationship between spouses is the heart of their whole life together. Prayer is at the *heart* of a life of faith; it is not apart from, or in opposition to, the other aspects of that life. Discovering the link between formal prayer and the "marketplace" dimension of our lives is precisely what we mean by discernment.[3] Thus the spiritual director's work is one of discernment.

But note that Barry and Connolly speak of direction as "help given by one Christian to another, which enables that person (the directee) to pay attention to God's personal communication to him or her." And Wright says, in a similar vein, that "one person assists another to develop and come to maturity in the life of the spirit." Both descriptions stress the helping, facilitative role of the director. The primary discerner is the directee herself. Just as it is her experience which is at stake, so too it is her discerning judgment, and her decision to act on that judgment, which is crucial.

How, then, can the director help the directee to experience God in her life, to understand the meaning of that experience, and to act on her understanding? We will come to that question, but first let us say a word about some other helping functions which are not spiritual direction.

What Spiritual Direction Is Not

In his monograph Wright says: "It will be helpful, I think, to recall some fairly commonplace observations to clarify what spiritual direction is not."[4] He says, first of all, that direction "is not primarily informative, although it may sometimes be the opportunity for supplying some kind of knowledge, especially . . . about the meaning of the Christian message." While my focus as director is on interpreting the faith-experience of the directee, it will often be necessary, in so doing, to clarify points of doctrine or morality: the church's teaching on birth control, our obligation to make restitution for stolen goods, the Christian responsibility to support the government by paying just taxes. I find I often have to clarify for devout married persons involved in a charismatic community the fact that their primary responsibility is to the spouse and to the young children. And when directing a woman in her middle years who is undergoing stress and unpredictable mood swings, I have to ask whether she might be passing through menopause. If so, she needs good information on the normal chemical and emotional changes of that time of transition. I often find she has not suspected that possibility, and I can refer her to a good gynecologist and recommend a physical checkup.

This last example, which occurs frequently in my experience in Manila, brings out a second point of Wright, that spiritual direction is "not primarily advisory." I do have to suggest a physical checkup to the woman in question. As with information, I cannot avoid giving advice altogether—even though that is not my primary role as a spiritual director. Since directees are often eager to get, and follow, my advice, I have learned that I have to be careful in the way I phrase it. That is, I do not want them to act on it simply because "Father said so." If they do, they will never come to mature personal responsibility. I can imagine on judgment day, when the Lord asks them why they did what they did, their replying: "I simply followed Father Green's advice. He is responsible for any fault there may be!" I would fear judgment day myself—or, more likely, be afraid to give *any* advice—if I thought that were true!

At times it is necessary to provide information and to give advice, but the director should not take responsibility for the directee's life. He or she should not make decisions for her. We will see in Chapter Four that John of the Cross considers this the great failing of most directors. For me, the best way to avoid this failing is to say: "If I were in your situation, I would consult a good gynecologist." Or, "If I were you, I would not continue a relationship with a person who cannot hold a steady job. But the decision is yours. I am not you, so I can only tell you what I would do if I were." And then I have to respect her decision, and not say (or imply), "Why did you not do what I told you?"

Finally, Wright says that spiritual direction "is not primarily therapeutic, though therapy, of course, may be called for in some cases. Psychological illness, if it is at all serious, needs someone who is trained professionally to handle such problems." I am not a trained psychologist, and am grateful that I am not—not because I do not value psychology, but because I think it would be killing to wear both hats at the same time. (Fortunately, there is an excellent "Center for Family Ministry"—CEFAM— with very competent counselors and psychologists within one hundred yards/meters of San Jose Seminary.) As the years pass, I can handle the more ordinary problems (like menopause) as they normally occur, but I do not want to play with, or experiment with, a person's psyche. When there are more than ordinary problems in this area, I do have to provide information (for example, that menopausal anxiety does not sound to me like the dark night) and advice (particularly, to suggest that the directee seek help, and to be able to give her the names of persons who, in my judgment, can help her).

Similar but Distinct: Spiritual Direction and Pastoral Counseling

There is an area which overlaps the boundaries between spirituality and psychology. It is known as pastoral counseling and is the primary concern of CEFAM. As the word "pastoral" implies, both pastoral counseling and spiritual direction presuppose a faith context. Both are God-centered by definition.

It would be possible to consult, and be helped by, a psychologist or a psychiatrist who was not himself or herself a person of faith. They could help me to confront my problem from a natural, "scientific" perspective. As a trained philosopher of science, with a great respect for the autonomy and the success of science in its own domain, I could scarcely deny that possibility. But when dealing with the spiritual part of the person, it is often very difficult to tackle the problem purely from the perspective of the empirical science of psychology. That, I think, is why the hybrid discipline called pastoral counseling has evolved.

So pastoral counseling and spiritual direction are similar in that they both presuppose a faith perspective.

For that reason, Fr. Ruben Tanseco, S.J., the founder of CEFAM, has often asked me to speak to CEFAM students on the difference between the two. Basically, I see two important differences, the discussion of which can clarify further what spiritual direction is precisely.

In the first place, I see pastoral counseling as problem-centered (in a good sense), whereas spiritual direction is growth-centered. I go to a counselor when there is some block to normal functioning. Some years ago, for example, one of my seminarian-directees had a serious problem with expressing his inner self. Every time he had to speak about personal matters, he found himself unable to swallow. His throat closed up. After some time together, I felt it would be very dangerous to try to "spiritualize" his problem: to seek to conquer his more-than-normal anxiety by prayer and pious exercises. I referred him to CEFAM, and, with the help of a competent counselor, he was able to overcome his problem. In fact, he became a good and effective priest, and has held important responsibilities in his diocese.

This brings out a second significant difference between problem-centered counseling and growth-centered spiritual direction. The former is, by its very nature, temporary. That is, we go to a good counselor as long as is necessary to resolve our problem. But once my seminarian-directee had conquered his anxiety and was able to speak freely without choking up, he could bid a grateful farewell to his counselor. It would not normally be advisable to have a counselor for life. By contrast, since spiritual direction is growth-centered, and since growth is a life-long process, it does make good sense to have a spiritual director for life. The seminarian and I were able to continue our relationship, and to focus peacefully on the crucial business of growth in the Lord.

As I noted earlier, these two areas are closely related. In helping a directee to grow, I do have to help her to face her blocks to normal and happy functioning as a friend of the Lord. And as the years go by and my experience widens, I find we can tackle quite well the ordinary anxieties and insecurities which human beings experience. I also had a directee and a dear friend (she died not long ago) who had a problem—not with swallowing, but with talking about herself without crying. At first I was not sure what deep sorrows were behind her crying, but as time passed it seemed to be an involuntary reaction. There must have been roots in her inner self, but she could laugh about the crying, and it never prevented us from getting on with the business of her growth.

If she were preparing for the priesthood and would have to spend much of her life revealing herself to others, like my seminarian friend, I would have found it important to suggest that she seek counseling. But since she was already retired from a responsible position in the business world, and since she was able to deal with— even laugh at—her tearfulness, I did not see the need to undergo expensive counseling.

As a young Jesuit, I was struck by the title of a book by an English fellow Jesuit, Bernard Basset. It was called *We Neurotics*.[5] Basset's point was that all of us have neuroses, irrational fears, and anxieties. As I tell my students today, if my neuroses are manageable—if I can live my personal vocation happily despite them—then I am "normal." Professional help is needed when my neuroses interfere with normal functioning. When I cannot focus on loving and serving the Lord because of some inner block, then it is important to seek the help of a competent pastoral counselor.

What Spiritual Direction Is

If the director is not primarily an adviser, a teacher, or a therapist, what precisely is her or his role? John Wright, in the monograph cited earlier, says: "The fundamental method of spiritual direction is conversation . . . (which) enables one to objectify, to conceptualize, and thus to understand one's own living of the life of faith, hope and charity."[6] In order to take possession of her experience, the directee must be able to express it to herself. The good director helps her to do this by being a good and creative listener. If she can make sense of the experience as she shares it with the director, then "the person will be enabled, in the light of this conversation, to discern the movements and the guidance of God in his (or her) life. He will be able to see the divine initiative of loving invitation, in which God is seeking from him some kind of response."

Thus Wright sees two essential moments in the work of spiritual direction. The first we might call "clarification by objectification." In the very process of telling my story to you—of putting it into words—I myself understand it more clearly. In fact, I recall occasions when seminarians came to me for their monthly direction sessions, and told me their concerns. As they spoke, I found myself at a loss on what to say. I did not know how to interpret their dilemma, or what help to offer. And so I just listened. At the end of an hour, they said to me: "Thank you. You helped me very much!" I was tempted to ask: "Could you tell me just *how* I helped you?" It was a mystery to me. But I kept my question to myself. The important thing was that, in sharing their confusion with me, they themselves had achieved insight concerning their situation.

Fortunately, I do not usually find myself in that mystifying and humbling role. Usually I, too, can see more clearly, and so help to clarify, what is happening to them. Wright says, however: "No one can really express in words the full insight, the complete range of experience that he has. Nevertheless, we can scarcely begin to understand truly what takes place within us, except as the fruit of trying to objectify it. The very inadequacy of our formulation helps us to recognize the mystery in which we are involved. . . ."

The second task of the good director is to assist the directee in discernment. "The purpose of this is not that the individual may determine the measure of his spiritual development, but that he may understand how he ought to respond to God." Discernment is, as I have said, "where prayer and action meet." Once I can name my faith-experience, the question inevitably arises: "What response shall I make to the Lord, for His goodness to me?"(Ps 116:12). Our Christian life is a dialogue of love. As I have explained in *Weeds Among the Wheat* (especially Chapter Four), we discern two things. First, who is speaking? Is it the Lord, or some contrary "spirit"? And second, if it is the Lord, what is he saying? What is he calling me to do or to think?

The important point of our discussion is that the primary discerner is the directee. As Wright puts it: "in the end, the man himself (the directee) will have to identify within him what really is the invitation of the Holy Spirit to which he is called to respond." A good director can be a great help in this work of discerning love. How? Wright expresses it well:

> The very objectification may make it clear which are the inspirations of the Holy Spirit, and which are delusions and deceptions. At times, however, it may be problematic and obscure. And then, I think, the director can be positively helpful, provided he himself is led by the Spirit. To render this kind of assistance, it is not enough to have bookish knowledge about spiritual things. . . . The director must have a real sensitivity to the Holy Spirit, and to the guidance of the Spirit in his own life . . . (including) some acquaintance with the normal pattern of the development of the spiritual life, especially the life of prayer.

I have described the director as a co-discerner, an interpreter, a "diagnostician." One does not have much confidence in a doctor who, no matter how brilliant he or she may be, is not able to listen to my description of my symptoms, or who lacks the experience to interpret what they mean. We will say more about this in the next chapter, in discussing the qualities to look for in a good spiritual director. Let me conclude this section, though, by referring to an insight of Fr. William Connolly, S.J., which has been very helpful to me in understanding the central role of the spiritual director.

In another monograph in the *Studies in the Spirituality of Jesuits* series, titled "Contemporary Spiritual Direction: Scope and Principles," Connolly says: "Since the goal of spiritual direction is a developing and deepening union with God, then the primary task of the director is to facilitate contemplation."[7] What does he mean by "contemplation"? As I had occasion to note in *Opening to God* and *When the Well Runs Dry*, this word has a complex history in Christian spirituality. Ignatius Loyola uses it to refer to the use of our imagination in the early stages of getting to know the Lord. For Teresa of Avila, John of the Cross, and most of the Christian tradition, it refers to the more mature stage of the life of prayer, the dark night or the dry well.

Connolly makes clear that he is not using the word contemplation to refer to "mystical prayer." He means it, rather, "as it is understood in the Spiritual Exercises." I have always been puzzled by this, as this seems to me to be a distinct, third sense. The important point, however, is the precise meaning he gives to the word. And he is clear on that: "When the directee has entered into a contemplative attitude; or when, in other words, the Lord readily becomes real for him and he lets himself be completely real with the Lord." God is no longer "he," but "you." That is the crucial moment, the turning point in a genuine spiritual life. I cannot say when precisely it happened to me, but I do remember the total change of perspective. When I entered the novitiate in 1949, we were required to pray for an hour in the morning and a half hour in the afternoon. I found it a very difficult time. We were given "points" to pray about, but I usually exhausted them in about two minutes. What to do with the rest of the hour? The problem was compounded by the fact we were required to kneel for the whole time of prayer—on battled-scarred kneelers which must have dated to the time of the first Jesuits in 1540! All I could think about was the pain in my knees. That and the deeply prayerful attitude of my fellow novices, since we were about sixty in one room. What had they found that I had not? My only consolation was found in gazing about the room and cursing them one by one! It was only years later (since we were not supposed to discuss our state of soul with each other) that I learned what the other first-year novices were doing: cursing *me*, because I looked so prayerful!

It is obvious that the Lord had not yet "readily become real" for me (or them). Fortunately this did not last forever. I cannot recall the precise moment, but sometime in those first long months I suddenly realized what prayer was all about. God became "You," and, at least in the consoling moments, I forgot about my knees.

Two Essential Qualities of Spiritual Direction

We have seen that the director's role is to assist the directee in understanding and interpreting her faith-experience of God. In this task the primary discerner and the one whose insight is crucial is the directee. We also saw that direction is not primarily directive (advice-giving, information-providing, problem-solving), although there may be occasions when each of these is called for. In my own work of direction, two further insights from the authors cited have been helpful in clarifying this co-discerning role.

John Wright tells us that the "relationship between the spiritual director and the one being directed is, in the terminology of Eric Berne and Thomas Harris, not a parent-child relationship, but an adult-adult relation-ship." What does "adult-adult" mean? Eric Berne, in *Games People Play*, pioneered a new approach to therapy called transactional analysis.[8] The transactions in question are interactions between persons. In analyzing the interac-tions, the counselor helps the counselee to recognize the various "persons" interacting within herself. Thomas

Harris studied with Berne for ten years prior to writing his own, now-classic *I'm OK—You're OK*, in which he explains clearly the parent-child-adult distinction.

> The Adult is principally concerned with transforming stimuli into pieces of information, and processing and filing that information on the basis of previous experience. It is different from the Parent, which is (quoting Berne) "judgmental in an imitative way and seeks to enforce sets of borrowed standards, and from the Child, which tends to react more abruptly on the basis of prelogical thinking and poorly differentiated or distorted perceptions."[9]

Harris's great gift is to simplify and colloquialize this somewhat technical description.[10] Following his lead, we could say that the Parent is the censor, the critic who measures our performance against set standards. The Child is the emotional reactor. When the Parent says: "Why do you always do poorly on exams?" the Child responds: "Poor little me. All the teachers are biased against me. Why am I always persecuted?" Each of us has within ourselves a Parent and a Child. The problem comes when the two live constantly at war, and there is no third party to arbitrate.

This third party is what Harris calls the Adult. If the Parent is the censor and the Child is the self-pitying emotional reactor, the Adult is the one who brings reason to bear on the transaction. The Adult says to both the Parent and the Child: "Let us be reasonable. It is not true that I *always* fail exams. Nor is it true that I am *always* persecuted." It is possible that someone does always fail, or is persecuted, but the Adult checks the facts first. And the Adult also looks deeper into why the Parent in me is so exacting. (Maybe my tortured conscience comes from over-demanding, unaffirming experiences when I was very young.) Or why the Child is so self-pitying. (Perhaps that was the way I learned to get my own way in my early years.)

As I said, each of us has within himself or herself a Parent and a Child—and, hopefully, an Adult. But the scheme can also be applied fruitfully, not only to the trans-actions within a person, but to those between persons. This is the situation Wright envisions in saying that the direction relationship should be Adult-Adult and not Parent-Child. If the director plays the parent to the directee's child—censoring, accusing, praising for demands met—then there will be no real maturing on the part of the directee. To connect this with Aschenbrenner's models of formation, we will then be in a novitiate situa-tion. The directee's whole focus will be to conform to—or to complain about—the director's demands.

If, however, the director refuses to play this game, and insists on relating to the directee as an Adult, then the relationship, if it survives, will have to be Adult-Adult. This is not always easy, as Harris makes clear.[11] Many directees, like many counselees, are initially look-ing for a Parent. A major Adult challenge for the director will be to help the directee to recognize this (clarifying by objectifying), and then to help her discern for herself how she should deal with it in an Adult way.

The second idea that has helped me greatly can be related to this need for an Adult-Adult relationship. William Connolly, in the same monograph in which he speaks of "facilitating contemplation," also says that the director has to make a crucial choice in her or his work of direction: whether to focus on strength or to focus on weakness.[12] He gives the example of a priest who comes for a directed retreat. He is a successful teacher and loves his work. The problem is that his community has begun to stress shared prayer. Perhaps they have become charismatic. The priest feels very uncomfortable with this, and uncomfortable in the community. Should he move to another community, still more traditional in their spirituality but a considerable distance from the college where he teaches? Or should he stay where he is, since it is convenient for his work, and tolerate as best he can the unpleasant community environment?

Connolly's point is that the director has a crucial choice to make. As his director, I can focus on the priest's weakness (his community problem) in directing his retreat. But if I do so, I will be playing the Parent to his Child, and the whole retreat will be problem-centered. And, to extend Connolly's story, if the priest decides to move to the more-distant community, six months later the leading charismatic will be transferred there also! If I enjoy problem-solving (and many directors do), I may be happy about this—since it provides a new problem, a new opportunity to be Parent, for next year's retreat! Problems are the middle name of life. They are Hydra-headed: when one is eliminated, two others surface to take its place.

What is the healthy way to help the priest in question? As Connolly says, focus on his strength. The director can help him to see that his real strength is the Lord's love for him, and his love for the Lord. This is the reason he came to religious life in the first place—and not for a congenial community environment. Once that is seen and experienced, he will have to face the problem, and he will have to make a decision. But his basic strength is clear, and remains his strength whatever problems the future may bring. As a mature man, he will be able to see these future problems in proper perspective.

Conclusion:
St. John the Baptist Before and After

In this chapter, I have tried to present my experience and ideal of the spiritual director's role. As a co-discerner, he or she plays a subordinate role: subordinate to the Holy Spirit, who is the primary director; and subordinate to the directee, who is the primary discerner. Connolly describes the director's role as "facilitating contemplation." As such, his or her role, while subordinate, is usually crucial. It is also a changing role, as John the Baptist realized so well. Before the Lord becomes personally real to the directee, the director's role is to bring her to the Jordan and point out to her the One who is preaching and baptizing there. After she encounters this Lord for herself, the director must have the sensitivity, the *delicadeza* (as we say in the Philippines) to fade into the background. The director still has a role to play, as we will explain in Chapter Five; but the friend of the bridegroom must have enough sense not to try to go on the honeymoon!

If this is the role of a good director, where do we find such persons today? That is one of the questions I am most often asked. In the next chapter, I will try to give my answer.

Question for Reflection and Sharing

Has my experience of spiritual direction (whether as directee or as director) been Adult-Adult, and has it been focused on strength? Also, has it helped me to experience God as personally real for me?

Choosing a Spiritual Director

In May of 1998 I was privileged to be the Conference Speaker at the International Anglican Prayer Conference in San Diego, California. My topic was prayer and discernment. Although practically the only Roman Catholic in a gathering of some 250 people, I was received most graciously by the audience. They were eager to hear whatever I could share concerning the Christian tradition of listening, discerning prayer.

Apart from my talks (one each day), the participants met in small groups to discuss various specific topics of concern to them. There was one other plenary speaker, Bishop John Sperry, the retired Anglican Bishop of the Arctic. He spoke eloquently and with great humor about the place of scripture in our life of prayer.

He had been sent from his native England, along with his wife, as a missionary bishop in the vast Yukon Territory. One pressing need he found was for a good Eskimo (Intuit) translation of the Bible and so he set to work with his co-missionaries to produce such a translation. One of the great problems they encountered was that the language of the local people, incredibly enough, had no word for "joy." When the translators came to the resurrection accounts (Jn 20:20; Lk 24:41; Mt 28:8), they had to search for an equivalent idea in the culture. The closest they could come to the idea of joy was "wagging the tail"! Thus it was that John 20:20 was rendered: "When the disciples saw the Lord, they wagged their tails." As you can imagine, Bishop Sperry's audience, including myself, loved this story. I used it, in fact, in my annual Christmas letter to my friends around the world in 1998, and they loved it too.

A good story is always worth retelling. I mention it now, though, because I see a link to the problem of finding a good spiritual director. At the end of the Conference, when the delegates graced me with a standing ovation, I told them: "I am truly grateful for your wonderful reception. I felt right at home in the Anglican family, and I received more than I could ever give. The only way I can express my feeling now is to wag my tail!"

Why was the audience so receptive to me? One of the great signs of vitality in the Christian community today is the desire, which crosses denominational boundaries, for a deeper life of prayer. The Catholic laity realize it is not reserved to sisters and priests, and the non-Catholic Christian communities realize that it is an essential part of their heritage. That sense had been lost for many Christian traditions after the Reformation. But today I find, as do many other directors, that non-Catholics are coming to us for retreats and for spiritual direction—and many non-Catholics, including some close friends of mine, are themselves bringing the tradition of spiritual direction back to their own congregations. We Catholics have been helped by the great non-Catholic scripture scholars of the past century, who trained our biblical theologians to a renewed sense of the importance of the liturgy of the word. And non-Catholics, in turn, are learning from us to appreciate Teresa of Avila and John of the Cross and Ignatius Loyola and other great prayer-guides, past and present.

This does pose a problem, though. One of the questions I was asked in San Diego was "Where do I find a good spiritual director? After listening to you, I feel the need for help to grow in my life of prayer and discernment. But such mentors are very rare among us." I had to reply that the same question is invariably posed to me by Catholic audiences. The laity feel that sisters and priests can find a director, but they cannot. And the religious reply (if I have a mixed audience) that they too find it difficult to get good spiritual direction.

It seems that good direction, like an Eskimo word for joy, is not easy to come by, whatever our life-situation. I believe, though, that it is not as rare as people think. But we do have to know what to look for, and this involves removing some misconceptions. Thus, in this chapter I would like to reflect on the qualities to look for in choosing a spiritual director.

As will be clear, I do not think it is necessary that a director be a priest, minister, or religious sister. However, providing good direction should certainly be a primary task of consecrated persons. One of the great blessings of the involvement today of the laity in the church's mission is that it frees its ministers for this primary responsibility. The apostles realized this at the very beginning of the Church's history. We read in Acts 6:2-4:

So the twelve apostles called the whole group of believers together and said, "It is not right for us to neglect the preaching of God's word in order to handle finances. So then, brothers [and sisters], choose seven men among you who are known to be full of the Holy Spirit and wisdom, and we will put them in charge of this matter. We ourselves, then, will give our full time to prayer and the work of preaching."

The major problem as I see it is that spiritual direction is a charism and not an office. All of us are called to pray. And every minister of the church has a mission to preach, for which he or she can be trained in the skills necessary to do so, adequately if not with eloquence. But spiritual direction is a charism, an art, and not a science. As such, it is not attached to any specific hierarchical office in the church. If one has the charism, she or he can acquire certain skills like non-directive counseling. No skills-training, however, will fill in for the lack of this charism. Moreover, no one director will be suitable for every directee. And, as we will see John of the Cross insist in Chapter Four, the time may come when even the good and helpful director has to recognize that he or she can no longer help this particular directee.

Granted, then, that direction is a charism, and that no good director will be ideal for every directee, let us return to the question posed by my Anglican audience—and by every group to whom I have spoken about spiritual direction. How do I choose a spiritual director? What qualities should I look for in him or her? Consider the following six criteria for making a good choice.[1]

A First Criterion: Compatibility

Spiritual direction is a friendly relationship. Directee and director must be comfortable with each other. We have seen that John Wright speaks of conversation as the primary method of spiritual direction. To speak easily with another about my deepest self, I have to be at home with that person. In the past when the spiritual director was seen more as a challenging authority figure, compatibility was not stressed. If I were a shrinking violet, timid and withdrawn, then a director who was a Prussian military sergeant was considered good for me. She or he would challenge me and confront me. My unease with the director would bring me out of my shell.

There is some truth to this view. At times the confrontation may force me to face my real issues. The problem, however, is that this approach is like teaching a baby to swim by throwing her into deep water. You may indeed get some good swimmers very quickly in this way. But you will lose many babies in the process! This can be seen in the story I told about baring my soul to my novice-master. His reaction, bowing the violin, forced me to withdraw into myself. There was truth in his reaction—and I have heard other classmates say that his approach helped them to mature—but I was not comfortable with the exchange. Our personalities were too different.

Fortunately I am an extrovert by nature. When I was a boy, my mother used to say (as she never had to say to my brother), "For heavens sake, keep quiet!"[2] And the story is told among my nieces and nephews that, when one of them talked too much, my brother called them "Tom." Given my personality, then, the hurt feelings did not move me to withdraw into my shell permanently. I wonder, though, about some of my co-novices. The same treatment by the novice-master could have had long-lasting effects in their lives.

The point is not that confrontation is bad. Rather, it is that compatibility of personalities is an important first requirement for good spiritual direction. In the Philippines we say that someone is *simpatico*—or, in the recent and vivid colloquialism, *kavibes*: vibrating at the same frequency, on the same wavelength, as myself. The conversation which leads to clarification and to discernment can scarcely prosper if director and directee are not *kavibes*. This is why, since we have very diverse personalities, no one director can be suitable for every directee.

A Second Criterion: Shared Vision

Closely related to the criterion of compatibility of personality is the need for a shared vision of the goal of direction. That is, the director must believe in what the directee is seeking in his life. In general this means his desire, as Wright expressed it, "to develop and come to maturity in the life of the Spirit," or in Barry and Connolly's phrase, "to grow in intimacy with . . . God." This is the "contemplation" of which Connolly spoke. A director who did not value prayer and discernment—not just theoretically, but in her or his own life-practice—would not be able to help the directee to a mature intimacy with the Lord.

This general point is quite evident. But the shared vision must go further. If my directee is a charismatic pray-er, I will hardly help him if I believe that all charismatics are crazy. I do not have to be a charismatic myself, but I do have to see the value of the road he is traveling. This has been important in my own life as a director. I am not, and never have been, charismatic. By chance I was a graduate student at Notre Dame when the charismatic movement started. Many of the early members were friends of mine, and some came to me for direction. But I never felt called to join the movement myself. I could see the value of it for them, but I sensed the timing was not right for me.

When they were joyfully praising the Lord, I had the feeling he was saying to me: "For heavens sake, keep quiet!" Not that the joyful praise was bad. I have often said that, if I had been born twenty years later, or if the charismatic movement had started twenty years earlier, I surely would have been part of it. As the author of Ecclesiastes said long ago (3:1-2, 7), "Everything that happens in this world happens at the time God chooses. He sets the time for birth and the time for death, the time for planting and the time for pulling up, . . . the time for silence and the time for talk." In those Notre Dame years, my time for silence had come.

Can I, then, direct those who are experiencing the "time for talking"? Yes, provided I can see the value of this time for them. I have always felt that the charismatic movement has played an important role in bringing late twentieth-century Catholicism back from the head to the heart. Our religion tended to be too moralistic, too conceptual. Yet Teresa said long ago, in the Fourth Mansions of her *Interior Castle*, that praying is not thinking, but loving—that the important thing is "not to think much but to love much." Of course, she goes on to say that "loving" does not consist in beautiful feelings, but in the greatness of our desire (our will) to love and serve the Lord.

I had to learn these heart lessons, sometimes painfully, from Teresa—and, I am happy to add, from my life in the very feeling culture of the Filipinos. Now I see how the charismatic movement can bring women and men to the same realization more quickly and painlessly. I can also recognize the importance of Teresa's distinction—for them and for me—between beautiful feelings and generous desires. That being the case, I have been able to help many charismatic directees.

What we have said of charismatic prayer would apply generally to the various callings and life-situations of my directees. Many are lay persons. I am not. But I do have a strong sense—expressed in *Come Down, Zacchaeus*[3]—of the value and beauty of the lay vocation, particularly after Vatican II. I can also see the beauty of the calling of my Protestant directees, even though it differs from mine. In fact, each of my directees opens my horizons to new dimensions of the Christian vocation: the priest involved full-time in prison-ministry, the banker who is a leader in seeking to bring ethical values to business and government, the woman in Australia (and two men in British Columbia) who are pioneers in the work of spiritual direction for the Protestant community. I do not have to have the same calling as any of them to be an effective director for them, but I do have to see the value of their calling. That is what I mean by shared vision. The director must believe in what the directee is seeking, and what the Lord is calling him to.

A Balancing Third Criterion: Objectivity

In Chapter Two we said that the direction relationship should be Adult-Adult and focused on strength. These two qualities underline the importance of a third criterion in choosing a spiritual director. While the director should be a compatible personality and should share (or at least see the worth of) my religious values, it is equally important that she or he can preserve objectivity in judging my situation. By objectivity I mean that I see the problem "from outside"—that I do not become emotionally entangled in it.

Compatibility and objectivity are equally essential. I find, in fact, that balancing these two is the real challenge of good spiritual direction. I become good friends with the people I direct. But it is a peculiar and challenging kind of friendship. I always have to maintain a certain "aesthetic distance." Otherwise I will not be of any help to them. Once I identify too much with their problem— if I begin to sob uncontrollably when they share their sad situation—then we have two people with a problem, and no one to help! At that point both of us need another director.[4]

My diocesan seminary work has helped much here. In my almost thirty years at San Jose Seminary, I have found that I do become very close to my directees. But I am always aware that they come from thirty or forty dioceses all over the country. When they finish theology they will return to their home dioceses. I cannot follow them around and hold them by the hand. If I do my job well, they should be able to stand on their own at the end of priestly formation. I am always there for them if they need me and I do care deeply about what happens to them. But I cannot make them dependent on me. Their problems and challenges cannot become mine.

The temporary nature of our close interaction in the seminary has also helped me much with other directees, who may live nearby for many, many years. Even then, as Ignatius says in his Spiritual Exercises (#15), the director should be "like the balance on a scale"—the pivot-point on the balance scale of his day—not inclining to one decision or another. The idea is to allow the Spirit to tilt the scale, without any interference from the director.

This objectivity is not easy to maintain. Since I do become good friends with my directees, I truly care what happens to them. And I do, normally, have definite ideas about what should be done. That is why I have to keep reminding myself that my task is not to decide for them, but to help them to clarify and discern what the Spirit is saying to *them*. To love dearly and yet to keep a healthy distance: that, in my opinion, is the real and essential asceticism in the life of a spiritual director. It also poses a challenge for the directee. He must realize that the objectivity, the healthy detachment, of the director is essential to his growth. For this reason, the relationship can also call for a difficult asceticism on the part of the directee.

A Fourth Criterion: A Good Listener

I said above that a healthy detachment is essential to good direction. Perhaps no word in the Christian ascetical vocabulary is so often misunderstood as "detachment." It conjures up images of an aloof, uncaring disinterestedness. Obviously, though, in the light of the first two criteria we discussed, this is not what we mean here. The director is a friend, one who shares my values and aspirations. But she does not make my problem her own. The director can, as it were, "look at it from the outside." That is essential if she is going to help me to view it objectively.

In order that the director preserve a *healthy* detachment, and help me to a more detached, objective view of my situation, she must be a good listener. This is implied by the first two criteria above, compatibility and shared vision; but it is important enough to merit further attention. Real listening is, I believe, a rare art among human beings. Often our conversations are cocktail party monologues. Each person is just waiting for the other to pause for breath, so she can begin her monologue. Or, if she is attending to the other person, she is planning her retort, her advice, her solution to the problem. To really be interested in what someone is saying, to be an attentive audience, is not easy for any of us. And yet, if the director is to be the co-discerner, assisting and not controlling the process of self-discovery and self-acceptance, it is essential that she truly listen.

This is a lesson which it was difficult for me personally to learn. As the stories of my childhood tendency to talk a lot make clear, I was not a natural listener. I did enjoy interacting with people, so in some sense I must have listened. But there was too much of me in the interaction.

What a joy it was, then, in my later years, to discover that I had truly learned to listen. It happened in a surprising, moving way. One of my directees—Sister Stella Rosal, S.Sp.S., to whom *When the Well Runs Dry* is dedicated—died on the very day in 1979 when the first copies of the *Well* reached the Philippines. She knew of the dedication, but never saw the printed copies. A week or two after her funeral, her provincial superior called me. She said that

Sister Stella had left a note with her prayer-journals, asking that I be allowed to read them before they were disposed of. I felt uneasy about this, not wanting to violate her privacy. But I respected her wish and read through them. I'm not sure what her purpose was; it became clear as I read, though, why the Lord wanted me to see them. One entry held an important message for me, which, because it refers to me and not to her, I will quote here. Sister Stella said: "My director is very mysterious. He just sits and listens, and doesn't say anything until I am finished. He merely helps me to work things out for myself." How I wished I could have shown that line to my mother and my brother! They would have been happy to see that talkative Tom had learned to listen.

Real listening is not passive but intensely active in a receptive way. It is much like the "floating" which I described as the goal of the "dry well" experience in prayer.[5] In fact, I feel that my experience of "listening" in prayer, of learning to float more gracefully in the dry sea of the Lord, has helped me to learn to listen to others. And my listening to them, in turn, has helped me in my dry prayer. In both cases it is important to listen to the feelings. Ideas are important, but the heart of discernment is in these feelings.[6] In the dry well, insights or ideas are rare. And yet something significant is happening at the level of the feelings. In spiritual direction, ideas are important—since we cannot objectify our experience without talking about it. But even more important is the way these ideas affect us.

Directees experiencing dryness in prayer often ask me whether this dryness is desolation. In itself, no. Dryness can be desolation, if we are disturbed by it. But the desolation is our *felt* reaction to the experience. One can also be at peace, at home in the dryness.[7] In that case, surprisingly, there is consolation. Similarly, in all the experiences we share in direction the crucial point is how they affect the directee. If she asks me whether it is God's inspiration that she enter a cloistered community, I have to ask what her state of mind was when she thought of doing so. Suppose she tells me she had just broken up with her boyfriend of four years, and felt, in her unhappiness, that it was better to withdraw from the world than to trust any human being. I would have no doubt that the inspiration to enter the cloister was *not* from the Lord. Disappointment in human love could be the trigger for a life committed to celibate love of the Lord. But to be genuine, the decision would have to be made in peace.

We see, then, how important it is to listen to the feelings. A good director must be sensitive to her own religious feelings, and have some experience in discerning their origin and meaning. She acquired this experience first as a directee herself, learning to recognize and to discern her own religious experience. Only in this same way can she help others in the work of direction, since the director is a co-discerner, and it is the feelings of the directee which are discerned.

A Crucial Fifth Criterion: Confidentiality

Spiritual direction, like the sacrament of reconciliation, requires strict confidentiality. The person being directed shares his inner self, his most personal possession. It belongs exclusively to him. The director has no right to use it in any public manner. I learned that lesson early in my Jesuit life, from one of my first spiritual directors. Perhaps I can share that experience by quoting some lines from the conclusion of an article on spiritual direction which I wrote in 1991:

> As I have long realized, the prayer lives of even those directees I know best and most deeply are still profoundly mysterious to me. I well recall the time when one of my earliest and best directors, the Jesuit priest and philosopher Norris Clarke, was transferred from the philosophate to Fordham University. We scholastics had a farewell party for him. And when it came time for him to say a few words, he said something like this: "I would like to thank you for many things these past years. But most of all I would like to thank those who trusted me to be their spiritual director. They were really saying to me, 'I do not understand myself. So I would like you to journey with me to the most private and personal core of my being. Perhaps together we can make sense of it.' And that is a tremendous act of trust. No matter how long I live or what I might accomplish, that is the greatest compliment anyone will ever pay me."[8]

Fr. Clarke's sense of the sacredness of the direction situation has remained with me all my life. When I came as spiritual director to San Jose Seminary, it was important to me to preserve the confidentiality of my seminarian directees. Fortunately the faculty agreed with me completely. Thus, when we evaluate the seminarians every year, it is understood that a man's spiritual director has nothing to say in the evaluation. This can be difficult at times, because as director I feel I know the man better and at a deeper level than anyone else—even his own parents. But the very survival of the direction relationship depends on confidentiality.[9]

There can be situations where it is difficult to remain silent. If a couple both come to me for spiritual direction—particularly if there is conflict or tension between them—the temptation can be strong to help one by using what I have heard from the other.[10] Or if a seminarian is approaching ordination and I feel it is a mistake for him to proceed, my sense of the good of the church can tempt me to reveal what I know. But I feel that, even in these situations, confidentiality must prevail. I may advise the spouse to tell her partner what she has told me—or the seminarian (or the sister in a troubled religious community) to make known to his superior the disturbing information he has shared with me. But if they refuse to do so, I must entrust the problem to the Lord. He cares more for my directees than I do. And he has the means to bring to light what they have shared with me. Fortunately, I am not God—just his instrument, to be used as he wishes. The problem, and the solution, are in his hands.

A Sixth Criterion, Ideal but Not Essential: Ahead of Me on the Journey

The five criteria already cited—compatibility; shared vision; objectivity; ability to listen, especially to feelings; and confidentiality—I would see as essential for good direction. The final one, being ahead of the directee on the spiritual journey, is not essential but is ideal. I say "not essential" because Teresa of Avila tells us that the two directors who helped her most were much younger than herself. One was Baltazar Alvarez, S.J., whom we met in Chapter One. And the other was the great John of the Cross, who was twenty-seven years younger than Teresa. She met him when he was newly ordained and she had already begun the work of Carmel. Neither John nor Alvarez had the experience Teresa had. And yet she says they were the two who helped her the most. Why? I believe it was because they had in abundance the qualities we have described above. They were her friends. They believed in her, and they were utterly discreet. In particular, I think they were not intimidated by Teresa, despite her being one of the strongest people who ever lived—and despite her reputation for holiness. If they had stood in awe of her, they would have lacked the objectivity, the healthy detachment necessary for a good director. And Teresa, despite her being a very strong character, appreciated their firmness.

The story of a more recent Theresa (early in the twentieth century) makes clear the danger of lack of experience in the director. No one doubts the sincerity or piety of Theresa Neumann of Bavaria. But there are troubling signs that she was, even if unconsciously, directing her spiritual director. A simple, devout parish priest, he tried his best to give Neumann good, cautious advice. He was concerned about her claims (largely disputed today) of regularly receiving the stigmata, and gently worked with her on these claims. But she believed that, while in a trance, the Lord spoke through her to the director. God told him (through her) that he was displeased with the priest for doubting the divine work. This frightened the director into acquiescence. Thus the troubling question: Was she directing him (through her visions)? Or was he directing her?

Whatever the judgment on Theresa Neumann, it seems clear that Teresa of Avila was not able to dominate her two youthful directors. But it was hard work for them. The story is told that Alvarez, when he was a much older man and Teresa had died, was visited one day by a fellow Jesuit. His room was filled with books—not unusual in a Jesuit's room today, but quite surprising at a time when printing was still in its infancy. According to the tradition, Alvarez said to his Jesuit friend: "Do you see all those books? Every one of them I read to understand Teresa of Avila!"

It is possible to direct someone who is ahead of us on the spiritual journey, but it is very challenging, as Alvarez's collection of books makes clear. If another Teresa came his way in his later years, it would have been much easier for him. By then, and largely because of his struggle to understand and help Teresa, he had become an authority on the interior life. At that time he could draw on his own experience, as a pray-er and as a director of others, in helping his new directee interpret her experience.

On a much humbler scale, I feel I am a better director today than when I was ordained in 1963. I probably had more book knowledge then, since I have forgotten many of the things I read and studied in theology, but now I have much more experience. Like other directors, I have developed a "sixth sense" concerning the ways the Lord works. There is, to use St. Thomas Aquinas's phrase, a certain "knowledge by connaturality"—a knowledge born of lived experience of the Lord and his friends, and not from reasoning or logical demonstration—which makes it possible to say: "That feels right to me." Or, "I don't believe the Lord would work that way."

Our sixth criterion, then, while not essential is very helpful indeed. If the director is a bit ahead of me on the journey to divine intimacy, she or he can speak much more confidently in helping me, the directee, to evaluate my own experience. And I will have much more confidence in her judgment if I know that she speaks from experience.

Conclusion: How to Begin

In this chapter we explored the question of how to choose a spiritual director. I enumerated six criteria, which I have gradually elaborated over the many years my students and retreatants have been asking me this question. Good directors, like good medical diagnosticians, are not very common. But, I have argued, they are not as rare as people often think, as long as we know what to look for. The first five criteria—compatibility, shared spiritual values, objectivity, ability to listen especially to the feelings, and confidentiality—I would see as essential to fruitful spiritual direction. The sixth—that the director be ahead of me on the journey with the Lord—is ideal, even if not essential.

There is one further piece of advice which I find important. Not infrequently a person seeking to grow in the Lord sees someone who seems like she would be a good director. Perhaps she seems to possess the six qualities I have described. How, then, should the directee begin? What is the first move? Surprisingly, perhaps, I would not advise that person to ask her to be his director. The relationship has to be tested by experience, before we can be sure the "fit" is good. There have been several cases where someone told me he thought he had found a good prospective director, only to have the relationship turn out frustrating or unsatisfactory.

What, then, should be his first move? My advice is to talk to the director who looks promising on a "one-shot" basis. That is, ask her if you can talk to her about some specific concern. It might be something Fr. Green said in his book which is not very clear to you, or something the priest said in his homily. If you do meet, and the chemistry is good, then you can ask the person to be your director.

As a matter of fact, this is the procedure I myself follow with new directees. Perhaps they have been referred to me by a mutual friend. Or they have read one of my books. If they call me to ask for direction, I always suggest that we meet first and get acquainted. Then, if both of us feel the vibrations are good, we can plan to meet on a regular basis. If not—if, for example he wants to focus on his visions and voices, and I do not seem to give them much importance—the directee can walk away without being embarrassed or feeling pressure to continue the relationship.

The mention of "walking away" raises another practical point in the choice of a director. What do I do when a direction relationship, which has been helpful, is no longer so? Is it sometimes proper to change directors? And what should be the director's reaction to such a move? Since those were important questions for John of the Cross, perhaps the ultimate "director's director" in the history of the church, we will consider them in the next chapter on John's "first blind guide."

Question for Reflection and Sharing

Have I found a director who possesses the six qualities described in this chapter? If not, can I think of someone who *might* possess them? (Recall the point in the conclusion about testing the possibility on a "one-shot" basis.)

4

St. John of the Cross and the Danger of the "Blind Guide"

In 1991 the church and the Discalced Carmelites celebrated the four-hundredth anniversary of the death of John of the Cross. As a Jesuit who wrote about, and greatly esteemed, John of the Cross, I was asked to write an article for the centennial issue of the American Carmelite magazine, *Spiritual Life,* and to give a lecture in the Ateneo de Manila St. John of the Cross Lectures series. In both instances, I chose as my topic John's teaching on spiritual direction. John is a many-faceted figure: the greatest poet Spain has produced, Teresa of Avila's stalwart companion in establishing the Carmelite reform, the authority on the mature stage of contemplative prayer which he calls "the dark night," and a theologian both creative and solidly rooted in the church's fifteen-hundred-year theological tradition. Thus, as is true of great historical figures generally, those who revere John focus on different aspects of his personality and different parts of his writings.

Pope John Paul II wrote a doctoral dissertation on John as a theologian and philosopher. For me personally—as a

Jesuit, a pray-er, and a spiritual director—John's major claim to fame is as perhaps the greatest spiritual director the church has known. *The Ascent of Mount Carmel* and *The Dark Night of the Soul*, read from that perspective, makes evident his gift for spiritual direction. St. Francis Xavier called Ignatius "the father of my soul." I would say the same, but I believe I have two fathers of my soul, the other being John of the Cross. That is why I chose, for the centennial article and lecture (later published), to reflect on John's teaching on spiritual direction.

The *Spiritual Life* issue in which my article appeared begins with an editorial by Steven Payne, OCD (page 66). He tells us:

> As his companion Eliseo de los Martires testifies, "John was fond of saying that the greatest vocation is to be a 'cooperator with God in the conquest and conversion of souls,' and that those closest to God 'consider it a small thing to go to heaven alone,' striving rather 'to take many . . . with them.'"

This expresses well the particular relationship I have with John of the Cross. I am eternally grateful that he cared enough to seek, by his writing, to "take me with him" on the journey—and to teach me how to care for others as he did.

There is a section in John's later work, *The Living Flame of Love*, which has greatly influenced my approach to spiritual direction. In the *Ascent* and the *Dark Night*, John is *doing* direction, with occasional side comments on how a good director should proceed. But in the *Living Flame*, Stanza 3 (paragraphs 27-67), he provides us with his most extended *teaching* on the art of spiritual direction. I try to reread this section every year, to keep me honest in my work as a spiritual director.

I first met John, however, when I was seeking to understand my own experience. It was about 1955 when my prayer became dry. There was a locked section in the philosophate library which we young scholastics referred to as "hell." It contained works considered dangerous to the faith, like Voltaire and Gibbon. And that was where John of the Cross resided! He was not considered heretical, but it was felt that his doctrine on "mystical prayer" was too deep to be understood by, or to be useful to, the young pray-er. My spiritual director allowed me to read John in my search for enlightenment about my own experience. The effect was traumatic. John's teaching on detachment and *nada* (that all except God is nothing) seemed to me to call into question my whole Jesuit vocation. If he was correct, what was I doing seeking, in the spirit of Ignatius, to "find God in all things"?

Many years later I would become convinced that John and Ignatius, despite their differences in temperament and terminology, were kindred spirits. At that time, however, I was greatly troubled. When I reported this to my spiritual director, Fr. Fred O'Connor, S.J., he said that perhaps I was not yet ready for John of the Cross. He was right, although what he said was a blow to my pride. I did obey him, however, and set John aside for some years. The darkness and dryness in prayer persisted; and at some point (I do not recall precisely when) I returned to John. I think it was always in the back of my mind that, if I was "ready," John could help me make sense of my prayer experience. When I later returned to his works I saw his teaching in a whole new light. He was not preaching a darkness and renunciation initiated by the pray-er; rather he was explaining, making sense out of, the dark experience into which the Lord had brought me.

The Value and the Danger of Spiritual Direction

I still had to realize that my prayer experience was far from unique. What John describes is the *normal* way God works in women and men who persevere in listening prayer. I was not "different" in some exotic sense. There were many pray-ers with the same questions I had; they also needed to hear his explanation. Many of them came to me for spiritual direction, and many more could be reached through books that translated John's teaching into contemporary language. To my surprise, a new calling (being a spiritual director) was opening up to me.

The Value of Direction

At first John was my key point of reference in understanding the dry well phenomenon, and in explaining it to others. Gradually, however, I discovered his explicit writings on spiritual direction, and he became my mentor there too. We noted above the famous and lengthy section in the *Living Flame of Love*. I discovered, though, that he also spoke of direction occasionally in his earlier works. In the Prologue to the *Ascent of Mount Carmel* (# 3), for example, John asks why devout persons do not advance in the spiritual life. His answer: "Sometimes they misunderstand themselves and are without suitable and alert directors who will show them the way to the summit."[1] And in Book II, chapter 22 of the *Ascent*, he says of those experiencing apparently supernatural revelations and graces, that they need "human counsel and direction." They should not rely only on themselves in evaluating these divine communications. "Whatever is received through supernatural means (in whatever manner) should immediately be told clearly, integrally and simply to one's spiritual director"(22, #16).

John gives three reasons why openness to one's director is essential. First, to confirm the "effect, light, strength and security of many divine communications"; second, because "a soul ordinarily needs instruction pertinent to its experiences, in order to be guided through the dark night of spiritual denudation and poverty"; third, "for the sake of humility, submission and mortification" (22, #17, 18). For confirmation, for instruction, for humility. While John's specific concern here is "divine communications" and the dark night, the values he attributes to direction are important, not only for one who has begun to experience the dark night, but for any sincere pray-er desirous of growing in union with God.

The Danger of Poor Direction

For John the story is not as simple, unfortunately, as the above comments might suggest. Since there are two human beings involved in the work of direction, the directee and the director, John insists that the pray-er must exercise great care in choosing a spiritual director. As he says in the *Ascent* (#18), an inept spiritual director who lacks discretion can cause great harm in times of consolation: by giving too much importance to the directee's "visions," by not guiding her to humility, and by giving her poor instruction because of his own fascination with revelations and extraordinary experiences like visions. None of these experiences, John insists, are necessary to holiness. And all of them can be produced by an overactive imagination, or by the devil.[2] John's way to perfection is always a "dark" way. Hence such directors err if they fail to "disencumber and divest" their directees of all desire for visions and other "mystical" experiences.

Fascination with the mystical is not the only danger John sees in poor direction. Lack of experience on the part of the director can also cause trouble in times of dryness. Many directors are "a hindrance and harm rather than a help" in times of darkness and desolation, because they themselves "have neither enlightenment nor experience of these ways." (Recall our sixth criterion in Chapter Three.) Some inexperienced directors will say "all of this [desolation] is due to melancholia or depression, or to temperament, or to some hidden wickedness." Again, "others tell her she is falling back," regressing, thus confirming her fear and belief that in some way she has really lost or offended God. Such directors, like Job's comforters, only increase the distress and suffering of the soul in the dark night of desolation.[3]

Below we will see that the harm done by incompetent or self-centered directors is one of John's major concerns in the classic paragraphs of the *Living Flame of Love*. Let us, however, end this discussion of his earlier writings on direction on a more positive note. John goes on to say, in the passage just cited from the Prologue: the good director realizes that this is no time for harshness and recrimination, when the directee is experiencing darkness and desolation. Rather it is a time "for leaving these persons alone in the purgation God is working in them, a time to give comfort and encouragement, that they may desire to endure this suffering as long as God wills."

For John of the Cross, direction is normally essential to growth in the spiritual life. God *could* work directly on the soul, dispensing with the human agent. But, as Thomas Aquinas said, the Lord normally chooses to work through "natural causes," through human instruments. At the same time, the director can become an obstacle rather than a help. He should be the instrument of the Holy Spirit, who is the strengthener and consoler of the pray-er as she journeys to God. There may be a need for the challenging word, but the good director must have great sensitivity in recognizing this need. Spiritual direction is both valuable and, in the hands of the insensitive, dangerous.

Two Moments When Spiritual Direction Is Most Valuable

John of the Cross (and Ignatius of Loyola) would see spiritual direction as helpful at every stage of the interior journey. We can never be completely objective about our own life-situation. For that reason, as we saw in Chapter Two, it is always helpful to be able to clarify and to discern our present faith-experience by sharing it with an impartial observer and co-discerner. As we mature, however, direction can become much less frequent; for mature pray-ers, I would say two or three times a year should suffice. Maturity means that we can do more of the clarifying and discerning for ourselves. But it will still be helpful to "test the Spirit" from time to time. A good director can affirm our interpretation of God's working, and can also challenge us to grow further.

Having written my Ph.D. thesis on evolutionary philosophy (in Peirce and Whitehead), I have long realized that the basic law of life is growth and change. Living beings cannot stand still. Either they are growing or they are regressing.[4] To pray the same way at sixty as I prayed at sixteen—or to love a spouse at sixty in precisely the same way I did at twenty-six—is a sign of stagnation. And stagnation is a form of regression. Thus the challenge is to stretch ourselves—or rather, to allow ourselves to be stretched by God—beyond the present. As Paul says in his letter to the Philippians: "The one thing I do. . . is to forget what is behind me and do my best to reach what is ahead. So I run straight toward the goal in order to win the prize, which is God's call through Christ Jesus to the life above" (3:13-14). And this is the challenge not only for Paul himself but for every Christian. As he says in the following verse: "All of us who are spiritually mature should have this same attitude" (15). To be a disciple of Jesus is to be "on the way," ever growing.

Good spiritual direction will thus always be valuable, at every stage of the interior life. There are two moments on our journey, though, when direction is particularly necessary: when we are just beginning, and when we move into the strange world of the dry well or dark night. A consideration of these two crucial moments can make clear the complementarity of my two "fathers in the Lord," Ignatius Loyola and John of the Cross.[5]

Beginners in the interior life need guidance because they do not yet know how to pray. This is the kind of person Ignatius had in mind in composing his Spiritual Exercises. The Exercises, in fact, began with the notes he made on his own initial experience as a convert to a life committed to Christ. He sought direction at the Benedictine monastery of Monserrat, and he learned much from his own trial-and-error experiences. When his search for God's will led him to Salamanca and then to Paris, he encountered many others like himself. They desired a more committed life, but they did not know how to proceed. Thus it was that he became the spiritual mentor in Paris of the men—like Francis Xavier and Peter Faber—who would be his first companions in the Society of Jesus. Being much younger than Ignatius, they found the theological studies much easier—and some tutored Ignatius here. But in the spiritual life he became their mentor and their guide. He taught them the ways of prayer which he had discovered, and he eventually led them through his thirty-day Spiritual Exercises, perhaps the first "retreat" in the history of the church.

Others, of course, in the church's 1500 year history had developed methods of Christian prayer for beginners: for example, the Benedictine *lectio divina*, the methods of eastern monasticism, and the teachings of the *Imitation of Christ*. Ignatius, in fact, drew on many of these traditions in formulating his own Spiritual Exercises. The important point, however, is that some guidance, some spiritual direction, is essential when one is beginning to live a new life in Christ. When Paul arrived in Ephesus on his third missionary journey, "he found some disciples and asked them, 'Did you receive the Holy Spirit when you became believers?' They answered, 'We have not even heard that there is a Holy Spirit.'"[6]

For beginners, like the neophyte disciples in Ephesus, spiritual direction will involve considerable information—about Jesus, about scripture, about the basic ways of prayer. At the same time, it will involve that self-knowledge, that self-confrontation of which we spoke in Chapter One. Once a solid foundation is laid, however, the primary need will be to clarify and to discern the pray-er's own experience of the Lord. And this brings us to the second moment when spiritual direction is particularly valuable: when we move into the strange and mysterious world of the dry well or the dark night.

This was the experience which led me to John of the Cross. If Ignatius is a master in the laying of a good foundation, John tells us that he does not write for all prayers, but for those who "as they are already detached from the temporal things of this world, will better understand the instruction concerning detachment of spirit."[7] He recognizes that others have written of the beginnings of a good prayer life. He knew Teresa's *Way of Perfection*, and was educated by the Jesuits in the spirit of Ignatius. His concern is with "prayer beyond the beginnings," when the night becomes dark.

This is the second moment when good spiritual direction is especially valuable. It is also John's main concern in the classic discussion of spiritual direction in the *Living Flame of Love*—although, as I hope to make clear in the following sections, much of what he says there would be equally relevant in directing beginners in the interior life. Despite their very different vocations, for both John and Ignatius the interior life, from beginning to end, is a process of becoming *free from* all disordered attachments in order to be *free for* finding and embracing the will of God in our lives.[8]

The Three Blind Guides of the Pray-er

In the *Living Flame of Love*, John of the Cross begins the lengthy digression to which we referred above as a classic source on spiritual direction.[9] He has been speaking of the way the pray-er moves through the various stages toward union with God or "spiritual marriage." And he has noted that, while all faithful pray-ers begin this journey, very few persevere, in this life, to the end. This leads him to say: "Oh, what an excellent place this is to advise souls on whom God bestows these delicate unctions, to watch what they are doing, and into whose hands they are committing themselves."

The Context: God as the True Guide of the Blind Soul

John then begins his discussion of the dangers the pray-er faces with a note of reassurance: "In the first place, it should be known that, if a person is seeking God, her Beloved is seeking her much more"(#28). Dark as our prayer may seem, we can find consolation in knowing that (as I have often expressed it) the very desire for God is a clear sign of his presence. We could not even desire God if he were not at work in us. What then must we do in this darkness? John puts it very simply: "The soul, then, should realize that God is the principal agent in this matter, and that He acts as the blind man's guide. . . ."

"The blind man's guide": this is the role of God in the dark night. The work of God is always mysterious from our human point of view. At this time, when the darkness sets in and love no longer follows on knowledge, the Spirit's ways are far beyond our normal human way of thinking and acting. It seems to us that we should be forming ourselves and others into good instruments, sensitive to the needs of the world we are called to serve. Good directors must remember, however, that theirs is primarily a work of discerning sensitivity to what *the Lord* is doing in the directee. They should recall that the principal guide is the Holy Spirit, and that we are mere- ly instruments for directing "according to the spirit God gives each one"(#46).

The Devil and the Self as Blind Guides

John's reference to God Himself as the "blind man's guide" leads him to warn against the blind leading the blind. The pray-er, he says, "should use all her . . . care in watching, so as not to place any obstacle in the way of her guide"(#29). How would it place an obstacle in the Lord's way? Only "by allowing herself to be guided by another blind man." And who is this blind guide who can lead the soul astray? John says there are three "who can draw her off the road: the spiritual director, the devil, and the person herself."

This is how John begins his discussion of the three blind guides who lead the soul astray in the dark night. What is remarkable is the relative amount of space he gives to discussing each one. He treats the second blind guide, the devil, in just three paragraphs (#63-65), and the third, oneself, in only two (#66-7). The remaining thirty-three paragraphs (#30-62) are a critique of the "blind" spiritual director!

The devil seduces the pray-er with the bait of sensible consolation and "some clouds of knowledge," when it should now (in the dark night) be content to abandon all its own efforts. "Abandon your activity, for if this helped you, when you were beginners, to deny the world and yourselves, now . . . it is a serious obstacle." As we noted above, John does value the meditative ways by which beginners come to know God. He would have little sym- pathy with the advice, sometimes heard today, that even beginners can simply center on a God they do not yet know.[10] We humans can only love what we know. Nevertheless, the time comes—and this is the situation of the pray-er whom John has in mind here—when the ways of beginners are no longer suitable and must be abandoned. We could say that the devil is a blind guide for beginners, by urging them to abandon meditative prayer before they have laid a solid foundation; and for mature pray-ers, by urging them to cling to familiar meditation even when the Lord is withdrawing them from it.

The soul herself is her own "third blind guide." How? She will also interfere with God's work if, thinking she is doing nothing in the dry prayer, she strains to perform acts with her faculties of memory, understanding, and will. John compares her to a child kicking and crying "in order to walk when her mother wants to carry her," or to someone moving a painting "back and forth while the artist is at work" (#66). I used the image in *When the Well Runs Dry* of a patient undergoing surgery, resisting the anesthesia in order to assist the surgeon![11] What, then, *should* we do? In the next paragraph, John tells us that we advance much faster when carried by God than when walking by ourselves—even though we don't sense God's pace or feel his movement (#67). Hence, once the darkness of prayer sets in, we must simply abandon ourselves into the divine hands.

The Worst Blind Guide: The Spiritual Director

We noted earlier that John of the Cross devotes three paragraphs to the devil, two to the self, and thirty-three to the first, and worst, blind guide: the spiritual director. Not only is his treatment lengthy, he is also quite irate.

Those who think of John as meek and mild, as living on some cotton-candy cloud, should read these pages to see how mistaken they are. These paragraphs (30-62) are the ones I reread every year, to keep myself honest in the work of direction. In them, John notes three major failings of the first blind guide.

1. *Lack of experience.* John's main point in the first paragraphs of his discussion (30-31) is that a director can be a blind guide because she or he does not understand the ways of God, and so is likely to keep the directee to beginner's ways when the Lord is leading her to growth and purification in the dark night. To remedy this, John presents a brief catechism of the normal stages of interior growth (32-35), and then, characteristically, cites several scriptural passages in support of his argument (36-38). Then he explains why this "holy idleness and solitude" (39) are an inestimable blessing despite all appearances. It withdraws us from all that is not God, through "a weariness with all creatures and the world," and draws us to solitude.

2. *Lack of sensitivity.* The director may be experienced and still be insensitive to what is happening in the life of the directee. In this case he has not learned from his own experience, or from the experience of his directees. Hence the danger. The insensitive director will agree with the pray-er that she is wasting her time, and so encourage her to avoid this "doing nothing" through forced acts of meditation and devotion. In this way, he destroys the soul's recollection and causes her distraction (42-44). John says that, unfortunately, such directors are the norm rather than the exception. "Scarcely any spiritual director will be found who does not cause [this harm] in souls whom God is beginning to recollect in this

manner." They are "like a blacksmith [who] knows no more than to hammer and pound with the faculties"(43). And what is the result? All the soul's "efforts are like hammering the horseshoe rather than the nail; . . . on the one hand he does harm, and on the other he receives no profit"(45).

We saw earlier in this chapter that, even in the Prologue to the *Ascent* (#5), John stressed the need for great sensitivity on the part of the director. She or he must know when to challenge and when to console. In times of darkness, comfort and encouragement are needed. In times of complacency the director must be more challenging. Harshness, it seems, is never John's way. But at times firmness is necessary. I find it a challenge to sense what my directee needs at this moment in her life. Her need, and not my preference, should be the deciding factor.

3. *Possessiveness.* Ignorance and lack of sensitivity are, for John in the *Flame*, two of the major failings of directors who are blind guides. Some "err with good will," since they themselves do not know any better (56). But others are more to be blamed: they act out of vanity, refusing to let the directee out of their control, even when another style of direction is clearly called for (57).

This last remark suggests that a director might well be helpful to a directee at a certain stage of her growth— and yet not be suitable at a later stage. What does this mean concretely? To explain the different stages of good direction, John uses the analogy (57-58) of fashioning wood into a statue. At various times we need a hewer, a carver, a "perfecter and polisher," and finally a painter and finisher. The hewer's role is "guiding the soul to contempt of the world and to mortification of her appetites." That of the carver is "introducing her to holy meditation."

These are the stages in which the soul is actively using her own faculties in prayer. Thereafter, the work is primarily God's. The good director knows enough not to interfere. "No man can do more with the statue than what he knows how to do; and if he were to try to do more than this, he would ruin it" (57).

For this reason, I have found it important to give my directees full freedom to change directors, whenever they feel it would be helpful to do so. This can be painful for the director, but it is the only reasonable attitude if our primary concern is the good and growth of the directee. Even those directors who err out of ignorance are still culpable, "for rudely meddling in something they do not understand" (56). But my sense is that John judges most harshly those who seek to possess the souls of their directees.

In Chapter Two we referred to Fr. William Connolly's monograph, "Contemporary Spiritual Direction: Scope and Principles."[12] Towards the end of his discussion of the role of the director (page 118), Connolly asks: "What then can the director implicitly ask of the directee, without running the risk of interfering with the contemplative process?"[13] His answer, I believe, is very much in the spirit of John's remarks on possessiveness. "It seems to me that he can only ask a development in freedom; that is, that the directee move towards greater freedom to let the Lord be Himself with him, and to be himself with the Lord." If he or she demands anything more, "he does so at the risk of confusing his own expectations with those of the Spirit."

Several lines further on, Connolly confronts the fact that the directee herself must make the choice for freedom. "This is a pragmatic expectation. The director does not ask the directee to be more free than (he) wants to be. . . . If the directee does not want more freedom at this point in his life, he must at least exercise his freedom by terminating the direction. . . ." Thus a directee might feel that I, her present director, can no longer help her. Or, she may decide that she does not want to pay the price, at least at this point in her life. Again, I as director may realize that the relationship is not productive of growth in freedom. Whatever the case, both of us have to be able to let go of a relationship that is not leading to a greater, freer love of the Lord. This is often painful. But the objectivity which we described in Chapter Three as the third quality of a good director, demands of the director the freedom to let go.

The Portrait of the Good Guide

John of the Cross's "first blind guide" is the spiritual director. Such directors can fail—be blind—because of lack of personal experience or because of insensitivity, or because they seek to possess their directees as their personal project or possession. Often, John says, they seek to mold their directees according to their own spirituality. The example I often use is this: If they are devotees of the Holy Feet of Jesus, then all of their directees must be "Footites." In the next chapter we will see how different this is from the way of the great John the Baptist.

John of the Cross's specific concern, in this famous passage from *The Living Flame of Love* on the three blind guides, is the pray-er experiencing the dark night of contemplation. But his essential teaching is applicable at every stage of the work of direction. This is clear from our discussion of the three failings of the first blind guide, the spiritual director. We see there what any good director, at any stage in the directee's life with the Lord, should avoid. As we conclude our discussion of John of the Cross's teaching, however, let us end on a positive note. What is the profile of the good spiritual director? How should she or he act? First of all, John says (#59), he realizes that "God leads each one along different paths." Don't, therefore, "tyrannize souls and deprive them of their freedom, and (don't) make yourself the judge of the breadth of the evangelical doctrine." Live in awe of the mystery of God, accomplishing his unique design in each human being. Don't, we might say, judge the whole elephant from the one small part that you—the Buddha's blind man—are able to touch.[14]

John develops a positive picture of the good guide in occasional comments throughout his discussion. Particularly beautiful are #46-47:

> Let such guides of the soul as these take heed . . . that the principal agent and guide and mover of souls in this matter is not the director, but the Holy Spirit . . . ; and that they themselves are only instruments to lead souls to the way of perfection . . . , according to the spirit that God is giving to each one. Let them . . . see if they know the way by which God is leading the soul, and, if they know it not, let them leave the soul in peace and not disturb it. And, in conformity with the way and spirit by which God is leading these souls, let them ever seek to lead them into greater solitude, tranquillity and liberty of spirit, and to give them a certain freedom so that the spiritual and bodily senses may not be bound to any particular thing, either interior or exterior, when God leads the soul by this way of solitude. . . . This is to be understood, not only of the renunciation of all temporal things with the will, but

also of the surrender of spiritual things, wherein is included poverty of spirit, in which, says the Son of God, consists blessedness. . . .[15]

God, like the sun, is above our souls and ready to communicate Himself to them. Let those who guide them, then, be content with preparing the soul for this according to evangelical perfection, . . . and let them not seek to go beyond this in the building up of the soul, for that work belongs only to the Father of Lights. . . .

Conclusion

In Chapter Three, I recalled Fr. Norrie Clarke's farewell words to us when he left the philosophate. I told the story to emphasize the importance of confidentiality in direction. For many of us, he had been our spiritual director as well as our professor. Fr. Norrie's words touched me deeply at that time, forty-five years ago. And I am sure they capture the essence of John of the Cross's teaching on spiritual direction. Norrie was keenly aware that, as a director, he walked on sacred ground. He concluded his farewell by saying: "No matter how long I live or what I might accomplish, that is the greatest compliment anyone will ever pay me."

As I have lived my own life as a spiritual director, and countless people have paid me that "greatest compliment," I have become ever more aware of the sacred responsibility it entails. "Set my people free," the Lord says. "Free from themselves and their fears and attachments. Free from you, the director. Free from all that is not God. Set them free to journey into the darkness that is light—free to find me, their Love." That, in essence, is John of the Cross's classic teaching on spiritual direction.

Question for Reflection and Sharing

Which of the "three blind guides" have I encountered on my spiritual journey? How have they led me astray? Have I learned from my experience of them?

The True Friend of the Bridegroom

In Chapter Four we considered John of the Cross's vision of spiritual direction. I said that, in my judgment, John is perhaps the best spiritual director the Church has known. That is a strong claim to make. In support of it we considered John's teaching on direction: he sees it as invaluable for any person who wishes to grow in the love of God. At the same time, he recognizes the dangers of bad or incompetent direction. Indeed, as we said, he would see the director as the worst of the "three blind guides"—the others being the devil and oneself. Ignorance of the gospel way to divine union and lack of sensitivity to the uniquely personal aspect of Jesus' formation of the disciples can make direction unfruitful and even harmful. The fundamental challenge facing the director, however, is to free the directee to encounter God in *his* experience. The director must not fit the directee into her own mold, or make her own experience the measure of his. Possessiveness is a great temptation for the director. But the directee is not my possession. He is not my project, but God's.

Because this for me is the central insight of John of the Cross on spiritual direction, I have long seen him as a kindred spirit of John the Baptist. The Baptist is very clear about his own role. He calls himself, in the passage which suggested the title of this book (Jn 3:29), "the bridegroom's friend." What does that imply? In the following sections we will explore John the Baptist's guiding vision in living his own mission. First, though, let me share a personal story which has made the Baptist's selflessness much clearer to me.

In the years following the death of my father in 1973, I occasionally came to the United States for lectures and retreats, or to write a book. When in Rochester I stayed with my mother, at our family home and later in her apartment. She was my best friend, and we loved to reminisce on the good old days with my dad. It was a joy to me to hear again the stories of their meeting, their wedding, and their early years together during the depression, when my brother and I were toddlers. One of my favorite stories was about their honeymoon.[1]

My mother was the only girl in a family of four. Her mother died in 1923, when Mom was about sixteen. Since her ancestors on both sides were Irish, the family, and especially her three brothers, were great jokers. My dad's ancestry, by contrast, was half German—and even his Irish father, like my dad himself, was a quiet, gentle, serious man. As the date of my parents' wedding came closer, my mom's brothers approached my dad to tell him of their plans for the honeymoon. They said that my mom was their only sister, and no longer had her mother to look after her. And so they felt it their responsibility to care for her properly. Because of this, they told my dad, they planned to go with them on their honeymoon!

My parents were going to honeymoon in Bermuda; in those days, that meant a train trip to New York City to board the Bermuda cruise ship.

My dad loved a good joke, but it had to be clearly labeled as such. So he assumed the brothers were serious. They told him they knew he and my mom would want to be alone on their wedding night, so they would take a different train to New York City and meet them at the ship. In my dad's world, one did not jest about such things. He was a nervous wreck as he and my mother traveled to New York. My mom said she knew her brothers to be teasers, so she was pretty sure they were joking. But she also knew they were just crazy enough to follow through on their promise. It was, then, a joyous moment for both of them when the ship left New York harbor without any sign of the brothers—though I imagine my dad checked the ship thoroughly before he relaxed!

John the Baptist: Messiah or Elijah?

The story of my parents' honeymoon has helped me to understand the real greatness of John the Baptist. He is very clear about the role of the relatives of the bride and groom. While my uncles were not serious about their plan to join the honeymoon trip, many people—perhaps in more subtle ways—do fail to recognize the need for privacy which is the essence of a honeymoon. John, however, saw clearly and accepted—even rejoiced in—the fact that his calling was simply to be the matchmaker between Jesus and his first disciples.

In all four gospels, the messianic age begins with the preaching of John the Baptist. Three of them (the exception being Mark) begin with a prologue, which is like the overture to a symphony or musical comedy. The prologue states the main themes of the story to come. Matthew's prologue (chapters 1 and 2), which centers on Joseph, makes the point that Jesus is the new Moses and the church the new Israel. John the Baptist does not appear in Matthew's overture. In Luke's (also chapters 1 and 2), however, John's birth is given prominence since it is paralleled with that of Jesus himself. The Zachary incident and Mary's visitation to Elizabeth underscore both the importance and the subordinate role of John the Baptist in the story of salvation. And John's gospel makes the same points much more briefly (Jn 1:6-8, 15) in his prologue.

The reason for this stress on John the Baptist as a key but subsidiary player in the drama becomes clear once the gospel proper begins. In all four gospels the first act is John's call from the desert to preach a baptism of repentance in the region around the Jordan River.[2] The details of the stories vary slightly, but all four evangelists agree on the essentials. John (whose name means "Yahweh is gracious") is an austere and charismatic figure, wearing camel's hair and eating locusts, who preaches a call to repentance because the messianic age is imminent. He attracts great crowds, like famous evangelical preachers today, and many are moved to conversion of heart and to accept his baptism of repentance. At the same time, he provokes opposition and rejection from those to whom his message is primarily directed: the Pharisees and the Jerusalem religious establishment.

Because of his charismatic drawing power, many of his hearers begin to wonder aloud whether John himself might be the long-awaited messiah of Israel. Others suspect he might be Elijah returned from the dead. Why? A popular Jewish belief in Jesus' day had Elijah returning to earth as the herald of the messiah's coming. Since 2 Kings (chapter 2) recounts his being taken up into heaven in a fiery chariot, it was thought that he did not die. Hence the belief that he must return to the earth again, to die as the herald of the messiah's coming.[3]

Is John, then, Elijah, or is he himself the messiah? This is the point where his depth and authenticity are tested. And it is the point where he takes his stand as merely "the friend of the bridegroom." The success of his mission and the adulation of the crowds are an intoxicating brew. Many sincere evangelists over the centuries have begun well, perhaps as well as John, but then have been misled by their own success. They forget in their hearts (even while protesting with their lips!) that they are merely God's mouthpiece, the voice but not the Word. It happened to David and Solomon, who later repented, and has since happened to countless men and women lesser than they. It did not happen to John. This is why I see him as the model for a good spiritual director.

John's Understanding of His Own Identity and Mission

From the very beginning of his mission, John the Baptist seems to have had a clear sense of his role. Mark's gospel, as we noted above, has no prologue. He begins straightaway with the first movement of the symphony: the appearance of the one promised by Isaiah, "shouting in the desert, 'Get the road ready for the Lord. . . .' So John appeared in the desert, baptizing and preaching. 'Turn away from your sins and be baptized, he told the people, and God will forgive you'" (Mk 1:3-4).

Many came out to the desert to hear John, confessed their sins, and were baptized in the Jordan by this mysterious figure dressed in camel's hair and eating locusts and wild honey. Matthew and Luke have virtually the same account of John's appearance at the beginning of their symphony.[4] Writing later, and with other sources, they do add some details. But it seems clear that their basic source is the Marcan tradition.

Important to our discussion here is their agreement on John's understanding of his person and mission. Mark (1:7) says: "He announced to the people, 'The man who will come after me is much greater than I am. I am not good enough even to bend down and untie his sandals. I baptize you with water, but he will baptize you with the Holy Spirit.'"[5] In Matthew and Luke, John's proclamation is virtually the same, but Matthew, writing for Jewish Christians, adds a condemnation of the hypocrisy of the Pharisees and Sadducees. And Luke, with his typical concern for social justice, has John respond in practical detail to the people's question, "What are we to do, then?"(3:10) He tells each of the social classes among his hearers—the wealthy, tax-collectors, soldiers—how their baptism of repentance must bear fruit in their everyday lives.

John is courageous in proclaiming the word entrusted to him. In fact, as Luke points out, this leads to his imprisonment: "In many different ways John preached the Good News to the people and urged them to change their ways. But John reprimanded Governor Herod, because he had married Herodias, his brother's wife, and had done many other evil things. Then Herod did an even worse thing by putting John in prison" (3:18-20). Most of John's hearers were captivated by him, and even wondered if he might be the messiah. But when the prophet, like the spiritual director, is wedded to the truth, and to speaking the truth in love, she or he will always step on people's toes. That is the cost of being the true mouth-piece, merely the voice of the Speaker.

When we think of it, it is remarkable that John the Baptist, despite his great role in our story, had a very short public life. Mark tells us explicitly that Jesus began his own ministry only after John was imprisoned (1:14). This, however, is not the end of John's role in the drama. He is referred to a number of times by Jesus and by the disciples. And John the Evangelist tells us, in his beauti-ful tribute to John the Baptist, that it was the Baptist who sent the first two disciples to Jesus: Andrew, and an unnamed disciple whom the church has always assumed to be John himself (1:19-36). Even the Baptist's disciples were not his own property. Unlike the blind guide, John was not possessive.

It is John's gospel that expresses most beautifully and conclusively the self-effacing detachment of John the Baptist. In chapter three, after the encounter with Nicodemus, we are told that Jesus went to the province of Judea to preach and baptize. John was also baptizing nearby, and drawing great crowds. The proximity of the two evangelizers led to the following incident:

> Some of John's disciples began arguing with a Jew about the matter of ritual washing. So they went to John and told him, "Teacher, you remember the man who was with you on the east side of the Jordan, the one you spoke about? Well, he is baptizing now, and everyone is going to him!"

> John answered, "No one can have anything unless God gives it. You yourselves are my witnesses that I said, 'I am not the Messiah, but I have been sent ahead

of him.' The bridegroom is the one to whom the bride belongs; but the bridegroom's friend, who stands by and listens, is glad when he hears the bridegroom's voice. This is how my own happiness is made complete. He must become more important while I become less important. (Jn 3:25-30)

John of the Cross and John the Baptist as Kindred Spirits

The bridegroom's friend "stands by and listens," and "is glad when he hears the bridegroom's voice." That, I believe, expresses beautifully the stance of the good spiritual director. She or he must be a good listener, not only to the directee but also, and especially, to the Lord. But how, humanly speaking, could the director surrender the directee to the Bridegroom and still say: "This is how my own happiness is made complete"? Only if she or he— the director—has also found in the Bridegroom all that she is seeking. Thomas Aquinas said that "goodness is self-diffusing." If I have found my joy (my full joy) in the Lord, then I do not need to cling to the affirmation or appreciation or gratitude of others. I only need to share with them the joy I have found—and to rejoice in their finding it also.

One of my favorite scriptural verses is 1 John 1:4. At the beginning of his first epistle, John gives the reason for his writing: "We write this in order that our joy may be complete." But there is a magnificent textual problem here. Some manuscripts read "our joy," while others say "your joy." Which is correct? As John the Baptist knew, and as every good director must realize, it has to be both! Whichever the author of the epistle meant, his joy and the joy of his hearers are inseparable. Every parent who rejoices in the happiness of her children realizes the truth of this. There is, however, an important precondition: she must have found happiness in her own life—must have found her own center—if she is to rejoice freely, without any hidden agenda, in the joy of her children.

This is where I see the important connection between John the Baptist and the dark night spirituality of John of the Cross. When I was new to the world of listening prayer, it was Teresa of Avila whom I first learned to love. She was a marvelous guide when I was still afraid of John of the Cross. In those early years, she cushioned the impact of her demanding doctrine by her stream of consciousness style. She tended to ramble, partly because she was so busy with the work of reforming Carmel and had only random moments for her writing. And after her digressions she would say: "Where was I? I can't recall what I was talking about. And I am too busy to put things in order!" I never found her style threatening. It was a relatively painless way to get to the truth.

Teresa, though, is very talkative. And the time came in my life when I needed someone to tell me straight—to give me the medicine without all the coating and the candy. At that time I needed John of the Cross. In the years since, other pray-ers have often asked me: "How would I know that I would find John of the Cross helpful?" My answer, based on my own experience, is: "If you have learned to love John the Baptist in the gospel, then you will like John of the Cross. At that point he will be a good director for you. If, though, you still find John the Baptist intimidating, then I doubt that you will be comfortable with John of the Cross."

It is surprising to me that John the Baptist's name does not appear in the index to John of the Cross's writings. Apparently the latter did not himself see the connection I make here. But, based on my own experience as a director and as a pray-er, if the time in your life has come where John the Baptist's directness appeals to you, then you will find help in John of the Cross. If you feel that what you need now is direct, even blunt speech, then both guides will speak to you. Black is black, and white is white. Both Johns could be very compassionate and comforting, but not at the cost of glossing over the truth.[6] And both were clear that they were only the friends of the Bridegroom.

The important Jesuit spiritual directors in my early life shared that clarity. Fr. Norrie Clarke was a true friend. I never questioned his concern for me. But he confronted and challenged me when I faced the problem of integrating celibacy and intimacy in my early years. Fr. Fred O'Connor helped me, gently but firmly, to deal with the fact that I was not yet ready for John of the Cross. Several years later, when I was ready, Fr. Tom Clarke encouraged me to journey on in the darkness of faith. And when I came to San Jose Seminary in 1970, it was to help Fr. Jim McCann with the spiritual direction of the seminarians. The work of direction appealed greatly to me, but I was apprehensive. I was trained as a philosopher of science, and had virtually no formal training for direction. But Fr. McCann, who had been the Jesuit novice-master for many years, reassured me that I could apprentice with him. During my early years at San Jose he was both my own director and, informally, my supervisor. He taught me by example the importance of confidentiality. And he modeled the objectivity, the detachment, of a good director. He was, in fact, a Jesuit of the old school, and found many of the changes of Vatican II meaningful but difficult to assimilate. And yet he never tried to block me as I ventured forth into a new church. He could affirm in me what he found difficult.

John the Baptist's Dark Night

It now seems clear to me that I was blessed with several John the Baptists in my young life. And Fr. McCann's own struggle in the early 1970s exemplifies another important connection that I see between the two Johns. John of the Cross speaks of the dark night as the normal, inevitable way to divine union. In the gospel story of John the Baptist, he makes one more important appearance after his imprisonment.

Both Matthew and Luke tell us that John sent his disciples to question Jesus about his identity.[7] In Luke's version, Jesus had just healed the centurion's servant and raised the dead son of the widow of Naim. If he was the messiah, why was he reaching out to the Gentiles? The Jewish belief in Jesus' time was that the messiah would drive out the occupying Romans and restore the kingdom of Israel. Luke tells us (7:18-19): "When John's disciples told him about all these things, he called two of them and sent them to the Lord to ask Him, 'Are you the one John said was going to come, or should we expect someone else?'"

Many commentators over the centuries have said that John himself did not really doubt Jesus' identity. They felt his faith was too strong for that—and that he sent the disciples in order that *their* faith might be strengthened. The problem with this interpretation is that we have to read it into the scripture. Neither Luke nor Matthew suggests that John himself did not doubt. In fact, Jesus' reply to the two disciples is addressed to John and not to them: "Go back and tell John what you have seen and heard: the blind can see, the lame can walk, . . . the deaf can hear, the dead are raised to life, and the Good News is preached to the poor" (Lk 7:22). Jesus does not answer John's question directly. He does not explain why he is acting in this seemingly unmessianic way. Instead he pays a beautiful tribute to the faith of John the Baptist. Tell John, he says in effect, that the *fruits* of the messianic age are evident in my life. That will be enough for him. He may not understand, but he will trust.

John the Baptist is languishing in prison and is soon to die. It seems that he feared that perhaps he was mistaken about Jesus. If so, then his imprisonment and his death will be for nothing. As we noted above, Jesus is not acting as good Jews expected the messiah to act. Furthermore, after the two disciples leave to report to John, Jesus goes on to tell the crowd that John is the greatest of the Old Testament prophets, even though "he who is least in the kingdom of God (the New Testament) is greater than he." After this beautiful tribute to John, Jesus contrasts his lifestyle with that of the Baptist. In the whole scripture, this is the most revealing passage about Jesus' own way of life. It also makes clear why John would have doubted him. He begins with a charming metaphor (Lk 7:31-32): "Now to what can I compare the people of this day? . . . They are like children sitting in the marketplace. One group shouts to the other, 'We played wedding music for you, but you wouldn't dance. We sang funeral songs, but you wouldn't cry!'" Like children, they rejected the funeral songs of John's preaching. Now they also reject the wedding music that Jesus plays. What kind of messiah do they want?

Then follow the lines that reveal how Jesus lived. "John the Baptist came, and he fasted and drank no wine, and you said, 'He has a demon in him!' The Son of Man came, and he ate and drank, and you said, 'Look at this man! He is a glutton and wine drinker, a friend of tax-collectors and other outcasts'" (Lk 7:33-35)! John lived austerely from the day he appeared in the desert.[8] Jesus, on the other hand, seems to have lived a very ordinary life as far as externals are concerned. For John this would provoke a crisis. He expected the messiah to live as he lived himself—as the great prophets of the Old Testament lived.

Why is this important to our discussion of spiritual direction? John of the Cross says that the dark night is the normal way to divine union. He insists that all faithful listening pray-ers enter into the dark night. It is not the lot only of a privileged few mystics. What is special about the privileged few is that they persevere in this "purgatory on earth."[9] John the Baptist was clearly one of these few. Jesus' words when he sends the disciples back to John to "tell what you have seen" make this clear. His darkness in prison was his transforming purgatory, freeing him from all his own messianic expectations, and freeing him to see things wholly through God's eyes. Jesus is confident that the signs, the good fruits, will be enough for John in the darkness of his understanding!

It has been my experience that the purifying darkness experienced by John the Baptist is indeed, as John of the Cross says, the lot of all faithful pray-ers. One such faithful pray-er was a woman who first came to me for direction in the last few years of her life, after many years in the convent. She was a successful music teacher and had a very sensitive artistic temperament, which made community life extremely difficult for her (and for her companions!). If I had been her director thirty years earlier, I surely would have advised her that community life was not for her. But by the time we met, she was seriously ill and nearing the end of her life. She had no desire to abandon her vocation. What she did want was to live her final years in community fruitfully and happily. That was the difficult journey I shared with her.

I think she did find happiness and peace at the end— not by changing her personality but by surrendering her weakness to the Lord. What most impressed me about her was this: in narrating the constant community problems she encountered, she never told me what was wrong with the other sisters. Her concern was how *she* could live with them and accept them (and herself) more gracefully. That is why I was convinced that her struggle with her own temperament was John's dark-night purgatory for her. In accepting what she could not change, and in humbly surrendering her weakness to the Lord, it became the instrument of her sanctification. Like Paul, struggling with his weakness, she could say: "Three times I prayed to the Lord about this and asked Him to take it away. But his answer was: 'My grace is all you need, for my power is greatest when you are weak.' I am most happy, then, to be proud of my weaknesses, in order to feel the protection of Christ's power over me. . . . For when I am weak, then I am strong" (2 Cor 12:8-10).

I have lived long enough to be convinced that this is the pattern for all who are truly committed to the love of the Lord. Paul, John the Baptist, myself—each of us has our own area of weakness, which becomes in God's hands the sandpaper of our sanctification.

Another good friend and directee died some time ago. She was a professional worrier, a weakness we wrestled with for many years. I used to tell her (as I have told another friend and directee who could compete with her for the gold cup of worrying) that their anxiety liberated me from any tendency to worry myself—since they worried enough for both of us! Why are they close to the Lord, even though they could be difficult for others to live with? Because they accepted their weakness, and made it an occasion to surrender to the power of Christ in their lives. In the darkness they were able to let go, float free, and allow God to be the true Lord of their lives.

The Bridegroom's Friend After the Wedding

John the Baptist is clear that he is not the Bridegroom. But his role is nonetheless very meaningful to him. In the first place, he finds his whole happiness in the Bridegroom. While he does not go on the honeymoon of his directees, he is also the Lord's "bride": the Lord is equally *his* Bridegroom. That is why he can happily surrender his directees to the Lord: he has found all that he is seeking in Jesus. It is a joy to be able to share with others what he has found—and then to leave them to their own "finding." Because his happiness is now in the Lord, he has no desire to cling to his disciples, his directees.[10]

There is, however, still a role for the Bridegroom's friend after the wedding. Even at the level of human love, there will be times when the new bride is troubled by misunderstandings that arise. She loves her husband, but she cannot understand how he is thinking. If she and her mother have a good relationship, and if her mother is mature and wise and refuses to meddle, she can bring her troubles to her and gain insight into the different ways that men and women, even those closest to one another, think and react. When she realizes that her mother faced the same challenges at the beginning of her marriage, she can return to the struggle to make a good marriage herself with renewed hope. If the bride and her mother are not blessed with this kind of closeness, it will be important that she have someone experienced to whom she can talk.

The same thing is true in our love relationship with the Lord. While not interfering in the spousal relationship, the spiritual director is there if the pray-er does not understand what is happening between her and her Bridegroom. Since the director has more experience of the marital relationship between God and the soul, he can perhaps explain to her why puzzling things (like the dark night, or the death of a loved one) happen to her as they happened to him. Without meddling, he does care about her happiness—and, like John of the Cross with Madre Ana de Jesus, he is there if ever she needs him.

While it becomes clear as time passes and their relationship matures that Jesus himself is the real "director" of the bride, it is also clear that he often chooses to work through human instruments. This is the principle of sacramentality in the church. God could, for example, forgive our sins directly in the privacy of our hearts. But he told the disciples: "If you forgive people's sins, they are forgiven" (Jn 20:23). And Matthew ends his gospel with Jesus' missioning of his disciples to be his instruments in the whole work of salvation: "I have been given all authority in heaven and on earth. Go, then, to all peoples everywhere and make them my disciples: baptize them in the name of the Father, the Son and the Holy Spirit, and teach them to obey everything I have commanded you. And I will be with you always, to the end of the age" (Mt 28:18-20).

Why does he choose to work through human instruments? Not because he needs them; he could, in fact, do things much more efficiently himself. But, like the mother who asks the little girl to help her prepare dinner (even though it will be a much slower and messier process!) the Lord knows that the greatest dignity he can give us is to ask us to be partners in our own redemption. This is the basis of my hope and confidence in the work of spiritual direction. It is a joy to be the Lord's instrument, his partner, even though I will make mistakes along the way. He knows the weak person he is choosing. As long as I am sure that it is his choice, I can rejoice in his choosing.

All of the synoptics tell us that Jesus came to the Jordan to be baptized by John the Baptist. Only Matthew, however, says that John objected:

> At that time Jesus arrived from Galilee and came to John at the Jordan to be baptized by him. But John tried to make him change his mind. "I ought to be baptized by you," John said, "and yet you have come to me!" But Jesus answered him, "Let it be so for now. For in this way we shall do all that God requires." So John agreed. (Mt 3:13-15)

Even Jesus submitted to the principle of sacramentality. In his life—not only here with John, but also with Mary and Joseph—the Father chose to work through human instruments.

Conclusion: Journeying on "Alone"

As we continue to grow in the love of God, we will find that there is a limit to the principle of sacramentality. I spoke of some of the directors who helped me most on my inner journey. In later years, though, it became harder and harder to find someone to co-discern with me. This troubled me. I wondered if I was not sufficiently willing to open myself anew. But somehow I doubted that was the case. On one or two occasions, I did find a director who seemed promising—only to have the road blocked. Sometimes the problem was distance. On one occasion, though, I was just about to ask a priest to direct me, when he asked me to direct him!

Gradually I noticed this same pattern in the lives of others maturing in prayer and the life of the Spirit. A directee of mine might be transferred to a place where no good direction was available to him. I would urge him to continue to seek it, but meanwhile to trust the Lord. Eventually I came to see that this was the Lord's plan—that it was really good. At the end of his life, John the Baptist was alone in prison. That meant that he had to depend totally on the Lord to guide him. As I reflected on his situation, and saw similarities to my own, I realized that the dark night principle of our inner life applies equally to spiritual direction. That being the case, what guidance can we give to the pray-er called to journey on "alone"?

I would first explain to him that the human instrument, the director, is just that: an instrument. God normally chooses to work through such a person. But he is not bound to do so. Since Vatican II we are clear that Christ Jesus is the Savior of *all* human beings, even those in isolated regions of the world who have never heard of him. A century ago we needed a limbo, since we would have doubted that even the truly good among them could be saved. But today we know that God wills the salvation of every human being, and that he will provide the means to accomplish his will. The application to spiritual direction should be clear. I would advise the mature pray-er to be open to direction. Don't refuse it, but don't panic if you cannot find it. As we noted above, God may wish that, at this point in your life, you learn to depend totally and exclusively on him.

A second point of value is this: while formal direction may not be available, we can be helped greatly by scripture and by reading the great masters of prayer. I have made clear in this book and earlier ones that the masters who have most helped me are Teresa of Avila, John of the Cross, *The Cloud of Unknowing*, Leonard Boase's *Prayer of Faith*, and, for discernment, Ignatius Loyola. This is my own personal list. Each pray-er will have his own set of guides from the literature of spirituality. And many have told me how helpful it has been to return to the words of wisdom of their guides when face-to-face direction is not possible.

Finally, I would point out to the mature pray-er who cannot find good direction that experience is the best teacher. When we are beginners, we have the experiences but we do not know how to interpret them. That is why direction is essential for beginners who truly wish to grow. But if those early directors have been good co-discerners, good diagnosticians who were willing to give reasons for their diagnosis, then we ourselves should be equipped for the work of discernment as we mature. If so, then experience is indeed the best teacher.

We learn most, perhaps, from our mistakes. I often tell my seminarian-directees as they prepare for ordination: In your priestly life you will make many mistakes. "Mistake" is the middle name of life. They may be a blow to your pride, but they do not disturb the Lord—*provided* you learn from your mistakes. All I ask of you (and I am convinced it is all God asks of you) is to please make new mistakes, and not the *same* mistakes over and over again. If you do, that means you have not learned from your experience.

That is also very solid advice for the mature pray-er who finds himself having to trust his own judgment. If he is able to follow it, to learn from his own experience and his mistakes, then his director (the kind of director about whom we have been speaking in this book) has done his or her job well!

Question for Reflection and Sharing

In my course on Discernment and Spiritual Direction, I assign a reflection paper to be submitted at the end of the semester. Because of the personal nature of the topic, I can assign the same paper every year. It is based on C.S. Lewis's classic, **The Screwtape Letters** *(New York, Doubleday-Image, 1981), which is the correspondence in which a senior devil in hell (Screwtape) advises his nephew and directee, Wormwood. The latter is an apprentice devil, getting his on-the-job training in London. He writes to Screwtape concerning the problems he encounters with his assigned victims. The "Screwtape Letters" contain the diabolical "spiritual" advice of his uncle.*

I ask my students to reflect on themselves, and on how the devil can best work on them in the years ahead. Lewis's point is that the more we know ourselves, and our areas of vulnerability, the less likely we are to be deceived by the enemy. Since my students have found this exercise extremely helpful, perhaps you would also find it fruitful.

Hence our question:

Write a letter to your devil, advising him/her how best to handle you (as a director/as a directee) in the years to come.

Receiving More Than I Give

As I stated in the Introduction, friends often asked me, "Is this book intended for the director, or for the directee?" I envision it as being for both. But since the director, as we have seen, is an interpreter, a co-discerner, a diagnostician, I believe the focus must be on the directee. She and the Holy Spirit are the primary agents in the work of direction. Insofar as we concentrate on the director, it must be precisely as a good facilitator.

Perhaps, though, as I reflect further on the question, the real focus of this book is on the *relationship* among God, the directee, and the director. The relational perspective may capture best what we have been discovering and discussing. And it may express best what John the Baptist was saying. He is the *friend* of the Bridegroom, and the *voice* by which the Bridegroom speaks his word to the bride. He finds his joy, and his identity, in living this relationship fully and authentically.

What We Have Seen

In this Epilogue, then, I would like to focus more directly on the spiritual director, on what the direction relationship means to his or her life. First, though, it might be helpful to review, and synthesize, the main points of the preceding chapters.

Chapter One discussed the context of contemporary spiritual direction. Direction has meant different things at different points in the church's history, corresponding often to the diverse "models of the church" about which Avery Dulles, S.J., and others have written. As Fr. George Aschenbrenner has made clear, the essential model of direction in a post-Vatican II church is that of noviceship. The goal is the mature, personal responsibility of the directee. The good director must facilitate this inner growth.

Chapter Two, with the help of several respected contemporary authors, explored further what precisely this facilitative role means, and how good direction contrasts with (while sometimes overlapping) other legitimate pastoral activities such as advice-giving, therapy, and providing factual or doctrinal information.

In Chapter Three I suggested the qualities which I would look for in such a good director-facilitator. We saw that the question is: Who is a good director *for me*— for the concrete person I am, at this point in my life? Compatibility and objectivity must be balanced. The director must be a good listener, especially to the feelings, and be able to respect the sacred privacy of what the directee shares with her or him. It also helps much if the director is ahead of me on the interior journey, since he can then draw on his own experience in interpreting what God is doing in my life.

Chapter Four discussed the teaching of John of the Cross on spiritual direction. He was my own mentor in this holy ministry, and I found it important to show that his teaching—making allowance for the different world in which he lived in the sixteenth century—is in essential agreement with the points set forth in the first three chapters. John's special contribution to our discussion is his stress on the danger of the "first blind guide," the spiritual director. His particular concern is for the soul experiencing the dark night of mature prayer. The danger of the blind guide is present at every stage of growth, but especially at this time in that he tries to fit the directee to his own mold, his own spirituality. Thus we saw that John's teaching (like that of Ignatius Loyola) is very much attuned to the contemporary stress on inner freedom before the Lord.

Finally, in Chapter Five, we saw why I chose John the Baptist as the role-model for a good spiritual director. He sees clearly that he is only "the friend of the bridegroom." He acts as the matchmaker, and later as the confidante, of the spouse. But he is very much a secondary figure. What is especially beautiful about John's example is the joy he finds in his subordinate role. He shows us how the good spiritual director can be truly fulfilled being merely the voice by which the Word is transmitted.

The Risk and the Reward

In Chapter Three we spoke of criteria for a directee choosing a director. But what about the director? How does a person decide that this ministry is God's will for her or him? The work of direction is a sacred trust. How would one know they have been asked by the Lord to be the "friend of the bridegroom" for others?

One of my personal crusades in the Philippines has been to encourage more qualified women to undertake the work of direction. Our society is more traditional than that of the West. While it is basically matriarchal, there is still a sense that certain religious roles are proper to men, specifically to priests. Thus it is a joy for me that today there are several women whom I can recommend to others for retreats and for spiritual direction.

When a woman asks me how she would know this ministry is God's will for her, I tell her of the criteria we discussed in Chapter Three. Most important, though, is that she herself is solidly rooted in the love of the Lord. In this area above all, I can only give what I myself possess. I must have a strong prayer life. And, like John the Baptist, my prayer must be my love-relationship with the Lord. John's joy is genuine precisely because he has found in Jesus all that he himself is seeking. His own inner life is solid and strong. Christ is very real to him, as the love of his life.

Since direction is more a charism than an office, it is important to discover if I have that charism. I can consider the criteria proposed in Chapter Three, and see to what extent I find them realized in myself. But basically it is a question of testing them by experience. I always advise prospective directors not to advertise for clients— since they do not want to take this ministry by their own choosing—but also not to refuse the requests of others, unless they have a very good reason for refusing! And "Lord, I am not worthy!" is not a good reason, since none of us are worthy to be God's instruments.

Jeremiah, Isaiah, Hosea, Amos, and all the genuine prophets protested their own unworthiness. In each case, Yahweh made clear that he did not choose them because they were qualified. Rather, they were made worthy by his choosing. My favorite prophetic calling is that of

Moses. After his initial frustration with the Israelites and with Pharaoh, he protests in Exodus 4:10-12:

> But Moses said, "No, Lord, don't send me. I have never been a good speaker, and I haven't become one since you began to speak to me. I am a poor speaker, slow and hesitant." The Lord said to him, "Who gives man his mouth? Who makes him deaf or dumb? Who gives him sight or makes him blind? It is I, the Lord. Now, go! I will help you to speak, and I will tell you what to say."

Normally we do not receive the call to the ministry of direction in a vision, as Moses did. It is more likely to come through an inner sense that the Lord is asking me, through the requests of others, to serve him in this way. Then, like Moses, I must be willing to risk responding to the call. The ultimate test of my calling will be the fruits produced. If others are truly helped to grow by opening their souls to me, that is the clearest sign that the work of direction is God's will for me.

Since direction is a very personal interaction between directee and director, it is good to recall here the point I made at the end of Chapter Three. Even if I do have the charism for direction, I still have to determine whether I am the right person to help *this* directee. Thus I suggested beginning the relationship by testing it on a one-shot basis. Invite the prospective directee to meet once—particularly, as not infrequently happens to me, if we do not know each other personally—and to see if the chemistry is good between us. If so, then we can think of regular direction. If not, the directee (or the director) can walk away gracefully, without embarrassment.

At times I have felt that a prospective directee needed marital counseling, rather than direction. In that case, since I do not have training for marital counseling, I can refer her to a good counselor, without closing the door to future direction after her marital problems are resolved. At other times I may feel that the directee's whole focus is on visions and voices, an area in which (as a good disciple of John of the Cross!) I am not really comfortable. I can advise her, as John would, simply to ignore them. But she may not be prepared for that advice. In any case, it is her decision, and I leave her free to make it.

Receiving More Than I Give

As I grow older, I become more and more aware that my priestly ministry is a tremendous gift to me. And this is particularly true in the work of spiritual direction. I recall reading, in one of the publications of the Fellowship of Merry Christians, a wonderful prayer: "Dear Lord, make me the person my dog thinks I am!"[1] While our directees are more discriminating than our dogs, I can easily pray, "Dear Lord, make me the kind of person my directees think I am." Their loyalty and gratitude are affirmation enough for a lifetime.

I find myself thinking, though, "If they only knew me as I know myself." I look good to them because they do not see into the very core of my being, as the Lord does. I could be dangerously deceived if I judged myself by their gratitude. There are, however, some more certain and tangible ways in which I, as a director, am tremendously blessed, in which I do receive more than I give. I would like to conclude this book by reflecting on some of those ways, as I have personally experienced them.

In the first place, I find that my experience as a director has given me a much deeper understanding of God's ways with his loved ones. Most of us go through life wondering how others stand before God, compared to myself. When I was a Jesuit novice fifty years ago, I thought my co-novices were much more prayerful, more focused, more committed than I. That was because I saw myself from the inside, and them from the outside. I was comparing apples and oranges. The director, however, has a privileged vantage point. As far as is possible in this life, I see God working *within* the hearts of others.

As a result I have a much greater sense of God's fidelity and patience with all of us. I can see how in many ways my life—its darkness and its light—is similar to the lives of others. As a result I can better accept my own humanity, and be convinced that the Lord accepts all of us as we are. He wants us to grow, but he begins from where we are. And he takes each of us in our uniqueness. In God's world, I now believe, there are no universal concepts. We need them, that we may bring order to our chaotic experience. But for the Lord, each of us is a unique person.

This, then, has been the first great grace of my work as a spiritual director: a much deeper sense of the inner workings of grace, of God's love, in me and in others. A second gift is related to this. As I reflect on the lives of my directees, I come to a much deeper understanding of my own experience. My listening in direction heightens my capacity to listen to the Lord in prayer. Directees struggle with their human limitations. They find it frustrating that they are not able to love as perfectly as they are loved. As I discover this, the consciousness examen becomes much more an act of discerning sensitivity to what is happening in my life.

As I journey with them, I realize why the Lord leaves in them—and in me—these weaknesses of temperament and personality. If we were able to master them, we would soon feel sufficient unto ourselves. The life-long struggle brings us to true humility—in Teresa of Avila's sense of living in the truth. I see that in my directees, and that opens my eyes to see it in myself. In this and in countless other ways, my work of direction has brought me to a much deeper understanding of my own experience, along with a much greater patience with myself and others. As long as our heart is in the right place, the Lord is infinitely patient. Seeing this experientially, I can do no less than seek to imitate him.

A final great blessing of the work of direction is this: I find it provides me with the perfect justification to blackmail God! I remind God that he has to sanctify me, not for my own sake but for the sake of those to whom he sends me. Recalling Balaam's donkey (Nm 22:28), I often tell him: "Lord, you spoke through the mouth of an ass once, and you can do it again!" But I can only be his good instrument to the extent that I am shaped to his hand (*conjunctum cum Deo*, in Ignatius's classic phrase). It is a safe and legitimate form of blackmail, because what I am asking is precisely what the Lord himself desires. And I can be confident he will answer my prayer—for the sake of my directees.

Conclusion

Just as the spiritual director is the crucial person in the formation of good seminarians and priests, I believe that good direction is perhaps the greatest single need in the church today. We have spent far too long trying to keep people out of hell. That is, of course, a noble effort. But we may have failed to help committed souls to grow. All too often, our sermons and homilies may have been directed to the people who were not present to hear them. With good direction we can deepen the faith and generosity of those who are committed, who are listening.

This book, then, is essentially one man's experience of the great work of spiritual direction. In writing it I hope, of course, that it reveals universal values applicable to all direction. For that reason I have cited several other authors, classical and contemporary, whose writing seems to confirm my own experience. But ultimately it is my experience which I have shared. Paul and John and Peter were all very diverse personalities. Like them, I must share what I have seen and heard—and then leave it to the reader to decide if my experience rings true to her own.

> We write to you about the Word of life, which has existed from the very beginning. We have heard it, and we have seen it with our eyes; yes, we have seen it and our hands have touched it. When this life became visible, we saw it; so we speak of it, and tell you about the eternal life which was with the Father and was made known to us. What we have seen and heard we announce to you also, so that you will join with us in the fellowship that we have with the Father and with his Son Jesus Christ. We write this in order that our joy [and yours] may be complete.(1 John 1:1-4)

Notes

Chapter One

1. *The Autobiography of St. Teresa of Avila*, translated and edited by E. Allison Peers, Doubleday, Image Books, 1960, p. 311.

2. This course occasioned my earlier work on discernment: *Weeds Among the Wheat*, Ave Maria Press, 1984.

3. The article, unfortunately, has not been published. I use the version distributed by the CARA (Center For Applied Research in the Apostolate) Forum For Religious, #1234 Massachusetts Ave. NW, Washington, DC, 20005. Fr. Aschenbrenner applied the basic ideas discussed here to Jesuit formation on pages 150-152 of "On Formations for the Apostolic Life: The Novitiate," in *The Way, Supplement*, 29/30 (Spring 1977), pp. 149-154.

4. *The Long Black Line*, in fact, was the title of a fund-raising movie about Jesuit life produced at this time in the early 1950s.

5. My novice-master carried this one step further. He used to say: "If you want to find the roots of a good religious vocation, look to the grandparents." I think I can see the wisdom of his saying in my own experience and that of the seminarians I have directed.

6. This is the point of the "Calvary Darkness" of chapter 5 of *Darkness in the Marketplace* (Ave Maria Press, 1981). By then I had learned that my frustrating experiences are a normal part of the Lord's purifying process in those who love him.

7. This long-term bonding and friendship is particularly striking, considering that San Jose is a national diocesan seminary, with seminarians from perhaps thirty to forty dioceses all over the country. It is a joy to see how our annual homecoming in November is truly a "coming home" for men working in all parts of our 7,000 island country.

Chapter Two

1. New York, Seabury Press, 1982, page 8. Barry, in his later book, *Spiritual Direction and the Encounter with God: A Theological Inquiry* (Mahwah, N.J., Paulist Press, 1992), cites the same definition, also on page 8.

2. In the series, *Studies in the Spirituality of Jesuits,* volume IV, number 2 (March, 1972), page 41.

3. Recall that the subtitle of my book, *Weeds Among the Wheat,* is precisely: *Discernment: Where Prayer and Action Meet* (Ave Maria, 1984).

4. Page 41.

5. Bernard Basset, S.J., *We Neurotics: A Handbook for the Half-Mad,* London: Casterman, 1964.

6. Page 42 ff.

7. *Studies in the Spirituality of Jesuits,* Volume VII, No. 3 (June, 1975), page 114.

8. Eric Berne, New York, Grove Press, 1964.

9. Thomas Harris, New York, Harper and Row, 1967, p. xiv.

10. See Harris, Chapter 2, "Parent, Adult, and Child," especially pp. 34 ff.

11. See Harris, op. cit, Chapter 5, "Analyzing the Transaction," for many clear, daily-life examples of the various types of transactions (interactions) which may occur.

12. Connolly, op. cit., pp. 104-107. On pages 107-108 Connolly shows how the option for strength is basic to the Spiritual Exercises of St. Ignatius. This insight was central for me in writing *A Vacation With the Lord* (Ave Maria, 1986; revised edition, Ignatius Press, 2000).

Chapter Three

1. For an earlier version of this discussion, see my response to a question asked after my lecture, "The First Blind Guide: Spiritual Direction in St. John of the Cross", published in *St. John of the Cross Lectures*, Claretian Publications, Quezon City, Philippines, 1996.

2. In later years she told me that I started school early, not because I was bright, but because she needed a rest. She brought me to the public kindergarten near our home. When they told her I was too young (my birthday was in March) to begin that year, she replied: "Please take him. I am drained by all his questions!"

3. Ave Maria Press, 1988.

4. I think this is what happens when priests fall in love. Normally they are not looking for trouble. Most priests are sincere and committed men. In the course of trying to help someone, though, they allow her problem to become their own—and then fail to realize that they are no longer the person to help her.

5. *When the Well Runs Dry*, Ave Maria Press, 1979 (revised edition, 1998), chapter 6.

6. See my *Weeds Among the Wheat* (Ave Maria, 1984), especially chapters 4 to 7.

7. This was the point of my *Drinking From a Dry Well* (Ave Maria, 1991), the sequel to *When the Well Runs Dry*. In the earlier book I was speaking of the struggle to accept the dryness (desolation). In the later, the question was: Once we have accepted it and are at home in it (consolation), what is the Lord doing and how do we cooperate?

8. "The First Blind Guide: John of the Cross and Spiritual Direction," in *Spiritual Life*, Washington, DC, OCD Province, volume 37,#2, pp. 67-76. The quote is from p. 76; see also *St. John of the Cross Lectures*, Claretian Press, Quezon City, 1996, pp. 71-72.

9. For a very fine discussion of the church's growing stress on confidentiality, and on law as at the service of the dignity of the human person, see Kevin E. McKenna, *The Ministry of Law in the Church Today*, University of Notre Dame Press, 1998, especially Chapters Three and Four. Pages 37-38 summarize current church teaching on privacy and confidentiality. McKenna is the Chancellor of the Diocese of Rochester, NY.

10. This is why, in particularly difficult marital situations, I would prefer not to direct both spouses.

Chapter Four

1. The translation of St. John's writings used in this chapter is that of Kieran Kavanagh and Otilio Rodriguez, OCD, *The Collected Works of St. John of the Cross*, 2nd edition, Washington, DC, ICS Publications, 1979.

2. St. Teresa, in discussing nuns who were experiencing visions or revelations, advised her superiors to give them extra work in the kitchen. That, she said, would eliminate most of the visions they would encounter!

3. *Ascent*, Prologue, #4-5.

4. This is the insight behind the "stages of growth" in prayer which I described in *Opening to God* and *When the Well Runs Dry*, and which I tried to summarize in the Introduction to the *Well* (pp. 18-24 in the 1979 edition; pp. 24-30 in the revised 1998 edition).

5. I discussed this complementarity in *Drinking From a Dry Well*, pages 67-77 (Ave Maria, 1991). For the specific point made here, see pp. 73-75.

6. Acts 19:1-2. See also the encounter between Philip and the Ethiopian eunuch: "Philip ran over and heard him reading from the book of the prophet Isaiah. He asked him, 'Do you under-stand what you are reading?' The official replied, 'How can I understand unless someone explains it to me?'" (Acts 8:30-31).

7. *Ascent of Mount Carmel*, Prologue, #9.

8. This is the way St. Ignatius describes the purpose of "spiritual exercises" in the very first paragraph of his classic work.

9. Stanza 3, #27-67.

10. This idea is a distortion, not only of the *Cloud of Unknowing*'s original idea of "centering" (see Chapter 75), but also of Fr. Keating's contemporary teaching on "centering prayer."

11. Pages 110-113 in the 1998 edition; 107-110 in the original 1979 edition.

12. *Studies in the Spirituality of Jesuits*, VII, no. 3 (June, 1975).

13. Recall that Connolly sees the purpose of direction as "to facilitate contemplation." That is, to enable God to become personally real to the directee, and her to her Lord.

14. The similarity of John's image of the "three blind guides" to the Buddha's parable of the blind men trying to describe an elephant is striking. I do not know of any evidence that John was familiar with the Buddha's parable. But their point is the same: the elephant that is God (Reality) is too vast to be encompassed in the experience of any one human being.

15. Matthew 5:3.

Chapter Five

1. So as not to be haunted by my mom, I must note that she always said my stories improve with age and retelling!

2. See Mark 1, Matthew 3, Luke 3, and John 1:19 ff.

3. Jesus himself applies Malachi 3:1 ("I will send my messenger to prepare the way for me") to John the Baptist in Luke 7:27 and Matthew 11:10. And, in Matthew 11:14, 17:10-13, and Mark 9:12-13, he says that Malachi's prophesy (3:23–4:5 in some versions)

has been fulfilled in John the Baptist: "But before the great and terrible day of the Lord comes, I will send you the prophet Elijah."

4. Mt 3:1-17, and Lk 3:1-22.

5. Cf. Mt 3:11 and Lk 3:16. Also Jn 1:8-9, 15, 20.

6. About six months before his death, John of the Cross wrote to Madre Ana de Jesus, his directee and Teresa's friend. She had written expressing her fear that she would no longer have him as her director. In his reply he said: "I still fear they will make me go to Segovia. . . . But whether leaving or staying, wherever or however things may come to pass, I will never forget nor neglect you, because I truly desire your good forever." Kavanagh and Rodriguez, *Collected Works*, Letter #25. He cared for her, but the Lord cared even more.

7. Mt 11:2-19, Lk 7:18-35.

8. Fr. John McKenzie discusses John's affinity to the Qumran community of the recently discovered Dead Sea Scrolls. While McKenzie doubts that John belonged to the community, he says many of his disciples probably did, and his teaching and baptism and penitential lifestyle suggest a connection. Since Qumran is close enough to be visible from Jericho on the Jordan River, where John baptized, this is quite likely. See *Dictionary of the Bible*, p. 442 (Bruce Publishing Company, 1965), s.v. "John."

9. See *When the Well Runs Dry*, chapters 4 and 5, for my discussion of John of the Cross's claim that "this night is purgatory"—understanding purgatory, as John does, not as punishment but as transformation.

10. As a number two in the enneagram, I have found this insight especially meaningful for myself. "Twos" are professional helpers. Their compulsion is to find their self-worth in being helpful to others. Once I realized this, I could be a much more healthy "two." It is a joy to help others, for example in spiritual direction. But that cannot be what defines me as a person. The defining reality in my life is the Lord's love for me, and my love for him.

Epilogue

1. The Fellowship of Merry Christians is an interdenominational group, including Catholic bishops, clergy and laity, dedicated to proclaiming that the Christian message is one of joy. I first encountered them when I saw what has since become my favorite painting of Jesus, Jack Jewell's "The Risen Christ by the Sea." Later I came across two collections of "inspirational wit and cartoons" (*Holy Humor*, and *More Holy Humor*), edited by Cal and Rose Samra. The painting, the books, and their monthly publication, *The Joyful Newsletter*, are available from: Fellowship of Merry Christians, PO Box 895, Portage, Michigan, 49081.

LaVergne, TN USA
11 August 2010
192981LV00003B/16/A